Hamish Brown was born in Colombo, Sri Lanka, in 1934. As World War Two approached he lived in Japan with his parents, eventually returning to Britain by circuitous and dangerous means, as this book recounts. He is the author or editor of many books, a great outdoorsman and traveller who has made more than fifty visits to the Atlas Mountains in Morocco. In recognition of his services to literature, he received an honorary D. Litt. from St. Andrews University in 1997 and a D. Uni in 2007. He was made an MBE in 2001.

Also published by Sandstone Press

Hamish's Mountain Walk
Hamish's Groats End Walk
Climbing the Corbetts
The Oldest Post Office in the World and other Scottish Oddities
Walking the Song

As editor

Tom Weir, an anthology

EAST of WEST
WEST of EAST

HAMISH BROWN

SANDSTONE PRESS

First published in Great Britain by
Sandstone Press Ltd
Dochcarty Road
Dingwall
Ross-shire
IV15 9UG
Scotland

www.sandstonepress.com

The publisher acknowledges subsidy from Creative Scotland
towards publication of this volume.

ISBN: 978-1-912240-25-8
ISBNe: 978-1-912240-26-5

Cover design by Two Associates
Maps drawn by Helen Stirling Maps, Inverness
Typography by Iolaire Typography Ltd, Newtonmore
Printed and bound by Totem, Poland

To remember Ian,
entertain David,
and inform their families
and in thanks for our stalwart parents.

Contents

List Of Illustrations

Timeline

Year	International	Family
1893		Father born, Dunfermline
1909		Mother born, Bankok, Siam (Thailand)
1926		Parents married in Bankok. He, banker. Mother's father, engineer. Various postings in different countries.
1930		Ian, oldest son, born in Dunfermline
c.1932		Father posted to Ceylon (Sri Lanka)
1934	Hitler becomes Chancellor of Germany.	Hamish born in Colombo
1935	Japan over-runs Northern China. Mao Tse-tung's 'Long March'. Mussolini invades Ethiopia. King George V Silver Jubilee.	

1936	Edward VIII abdicates. Olympic Games in Berlin. Civil War in Spain. German persecution of Jews intensifies.	Long home leave, Ian left in Scotland with grandparents.
1937	Coronation of George VI. Chamberlain becomes Prime Minister. Concentration camps opened by Germans. Japan occupies Peking, Shanghai, Nanking.	
1938	Germany invades Austria. The Munich Agreement. Germany invades Czechoslovakia. Japan occupies Canton.	Oct - Colombo again.
1939	Spanish Civil War ends. Hitler-Stalin pact. Invasion of Poland. 3 Sep: start of World War Two.	Family to Yokohama, Japan. 3 Sep: Parents climb Fuji. Grandfather dies.
1940	Norway and Denmark fall. The Netherlands surrender. Belgium falls. Churchill becomes Prime Minister. Battle of Britain. The Blitz commences.	David born, Yokohama, Dec 15.
1941	June 4: Dunkirk. German soldiers enter Paris. Dec 7-10: Japanese invasion of Malaya. Sinking of *Repulse* and *Prince of Wales*. Pearl Harbour. Japanese invasion of Philippines, Java, Wake, Guam, etc. Hong Kong surrenders.	Family transfers to Malaya (Klang). Hamish attends school in Cameron Highlands. Dec 15: Air raid 'disturbs' David's first birthday. Dec 26: Family sails to Singapore, but father remains in Klang.

1942	January sees fall of Manila, Borneo, New Guinea and Solomon Islands to Japan. Feb: Sumatra invaded. Feb 15: Singapore surrenders. Mar 8: Java capitulates. Nov: Battle of El Alamein.	Jan 1: Mother and boys sail from Singapore to South Africa. Jan 11: Kuala Lumpur falls. Jan 7: Father reaches Singapore. Feb 13: Black Friday. Exodus of ships, most sunk, father's included, during Feb 15: Fall of Singapore. Mar 27: Father reaches South Africa.
1943	Allies land in Italy.	Family in Natal. Hamish at school: Highbury. Father moved to India.
1944	Burma campaign. Bloody Pacific campaign by USA. June 6: D-Day.	July: Mother and boys repatriated in the *Andes,* to settle in Dollar. Father in Madras.
1945	7 May: VE Day. End of War in Europe. 14 Aug: VJ Day. Japanese surrender.	Father in Calicut. Mother and David to Karachi. Ian, Hamish with Gran in Dollar.
1946	Cold War begins	Father to Karachi.
1947	British rule in India ends with the Partition of India	Father in Karachi as Pakistan is created.
1948		Father retires, family finally reunited after 9 years.

Maps

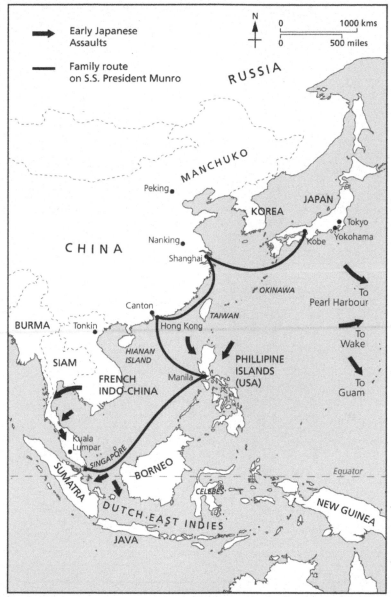

Early Japanese Assaults

Family route on S.S. President Munro

N

| 0 | 1000 kms |
| 0 | 500 miles |

RUSSIA

MANCHUKO

Peking

KOREA

JAPAN

Tokyo

Yokohama

Nanking

Kobe

CHINA

Shanghai

OKINAWA

To Pearl Harbour

Canton

TAIWAN

BURMA Tonkin

Hong Kong

To Wake

HIANAN ISLAND

SIAM

FRENCH INDO-CHINA

Manila

PHILLIPINE ISLANDS (USA)

To Guam

Kuala Lumpar

SINGAPORE

BORNEO

Equator

SUMATRA

CELEBES

NEW GUINEA

DUTCH EAST INDIES

JAVA

The Far East with Attacks Launched by Japan from December 1941.

The Malay Peninsula and Singapore 1941.

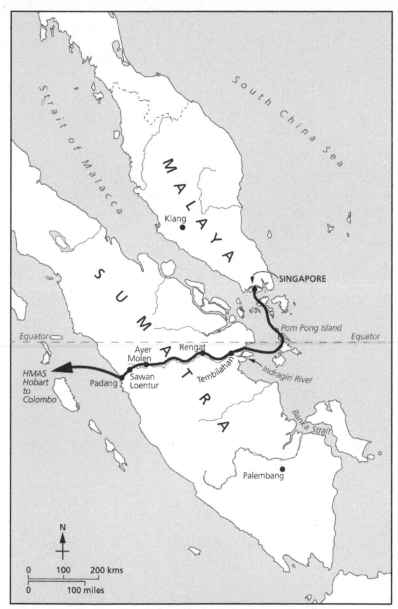

The route of Father's escape from Singapore.

Introduction

This is the story of one family's varying fortunes in Japan and Malaya as the world became engulfed in the Second World War. It is compiled from my mother's letters 'home' to Scotland, my father's notes and my own memories. The world 'east of west' is the least known part of that war, most people knowing little more than Pearl Harbour, the Fall of Singapore, and the Burma Railway horrors, but it engulfed every country on the Pacific rim. This was a world war within the World War. To give some clarification there are informative maps and a brief chronology.

I wondered about using the extensive description in Japan over the birth of David, coming at the start as it does, but female friends were emphatic that the 'period piece' had to stay. Without a new baby the story might have been very different. I hope I have used an adequate number of the Malayan letters home to portray the, for many, boring life many faced and, again for many, the almost ostrich's head in the sand blindness to the coming tragedy.

The 'chapters' of this story strike me almost like acts in a stage play, the script written by chance, fate, call it what you will. Before the curtain comes down on my own life I feel a duty to describe these now rare, at-the-time letters in

1

that grim time. The curious can read much more from the titles in the bibliography.

These letters, notes and memories are very much of the period as are my comments on them, but they are portraying what is now history while today's ideals and attitudes, mine included, have changed beyond imagining since then. So, don't be too judgemental. I was lucky to have had parents who were quite liberal for their time: strong, caring parents who must have borne constant concerns and, ultimately, very heavy hearts at a separation that could have been final. Life wasn't all privilege and fun.

Life could feel very isolated with 'home' a six week voyage away. Mother's letters only hint at the reality. Stiff upper lips had to be maintained and letters home clearly understate the reality, an astonishing understating in father's account of his escape. We are all children of our time after all and, in general, most people, then, now and everywhere, are doing the best their circumstances allow to lead satisfying, peaceful lives. Looking round the world today, with so many inhumanities, shows how little we learn from history. This book, if nothing else, will make us, you and me, realise how lucky we are.

Hamish Brown
Burntisland 2018

1

Family Briefing

My young brother David was born in Yokohama in December 1940. Big brother Ian and Gran were coming out from Scotland to join us in Japan 'for safety'. What befell thereafter is this book's matter. Father was not to see Ian for nearly nine years because of what happened. I can remember some things, recall what parents spoke of but am still wary of memory.

Autobiographical memory is variously portrayed as random, capricious, ephemeral, fragile, unreliable, elusive, non-sequential, impermanent, defective, treacherous, illusory even, which should scare off most from ever attempting such. Who, given a paint box, will produce an identical picture of the present, never mind the past, to that of a neighbour sitting alongside, looking at the same scene? That I take the risk is largely because this particular painting of the past is based on what was recorded at the time, something surely modifying the frightening words above?

A Chinese tin miner or a semi-slave worker on a rubber plantation would tell a very different story. They never did of course, the recorders came from the elite, the *sahibs* and the *memsahibs* and the pathetic rulers who failed in so many ways. I have my mother's pocket diary for 1941 which simply records dates for social events: riding, tennis,

Mah Jongg, shopping, dentist, hairdresser ... Nothing about the war in Europe and little between 'Dec 8: Japan into war' and 'Dec 26: Raid. Shop. Port Swettenham' – our flight. Whether pocket diary, or letters home, the outside reality never seemed to impinge on that world of everyday work and play in an unpleasant climate.

The very ordinariness of these letters written by a mother to her mother or to her son gives them a poignancy which no artifice could match. This is how it was *then*, for one family, however attitudes, beliefs and language may have changed since. Not that I feel anything other than admiration and gratitude for my parents, feelings deepened on reading their words.

East of West life continued with determined (illusory?) normality. There's an element of 'stiff upper lip,' of following what was proper behaviour, of protecting the children from the reality. Much is glossed over. The letters home were toned-down – but of course were opened and read by the censors. Huge events were happening 'at home': Churchill as new Prime Minister, Dunkirk, the Battle of Britain and the start of the Blitz (the last raising those thoughts that Gran and Ian would be safer in Japan!). Through 1941 father ran the bank in Klang, near Kuala Lumpur, mother socialised, I was sent off to school. The day the Japanese invaded I started school holidays and, a week before we fled, brother David's first birthday was celebrated as if life was normal. 'Shame David disturbed on his birthday,' mother recorded me saying. We children were protected from the realities as much as possible of course. Yet David was born in Japan, just a year before Pearl Harbour.

Tensions there were in Japan. Shortly after the fall of France Japanese forces had over-run Indo-China. Britain and America promptly froze all Chinese and Japanese assets. In September 1940 Japan and Germany signed a pact. The British in Japan became steadily more alarmed, many started to leave but the likelihood of real instability seemed to rest on Japan and China. An invasion of Malaya was inconceivable but with an embargo on coal, oil, iron ore, Japan in some ways was forced to attack, to keep going.

Memories can be tactile or olfactory as well as visual, which I have discovered on looking back. Often, though, so-called memories are acquired later through parental stories or looking at family photo albums, and I've my ration of such but can usually make a sharp separation between original and acquired memories. My very earliest memory is a case in point.

I'm standing on a pontoon, held by reins, with my mother in a port which I suspect is Port Said, on our way to Japan in 1939, and I am wearing a *topee (topi)* and shirt and shorts held together by buttons, the shorts green, the top white with large green polka dots. There was a photo of this scene but if the 'memory' came later I would surely have been told the name of the port and, while the long lost photo was black and white, my memory is in colour. However our memories drift like smoke to the other end of life, the constant is their random selectivity and having family letters pins down things with useful exactitude.

Young children don't question. They accept. Father as a banker and being moved about from country to country, one brother a world away and a new one arriving, was simply the natural order of things. My world was family, a secure enclave that needed no supplementing. It was all happenings, seen with 'the imperious accepting eye of childhood' (Penelope Lively). I was too young to be judgemental. I was lucky in having that strong family bond. I was not abandoned to *amahs* and *ayas*, my absence up in the hills was a parental grief, the days to my return counted by them, as much as by me. Constant change was our constancy. Memory still is elusive and their letters have been a strange discovering of myself as a boy.

Father was born in Dunfermline in Fife in March 1893, the youngest of a family of five: brother Jim (who emigrated to South Africa – usefully for us!), Helen (Nellie), who lived in Cyprus (and whom we'd meet in South Africa), Kathleen, whose family would be India-based, Margaret who married into Ireland and Eliza, the only one who never married nor left the family home in Dunfermline. The Brown name can be traced back in Fife to the eighteenth century but what fascinated me as a till then rootless boy, drawing a family tree, was how completely Scottish our roots were, and how far-distributed, in the Highlands and Lowlands as names indicated: Arthur, Brown (2), Dick, Fisher, Hunter, Lyon, Macmillan, MacPhail, Reid, Robertson, Swanson.

On leaving school father was taken on as a 'pupil' in the Bank of Scotland and appears to have had his call-up deferred to complete his training. He was enlisted in the Argyll and Sutherland Highlanders in 1915 and sent to the front where he caught a *'Blighty one'* on the Somme. In August 1917 he was commissioned into the Border Regiment but in the big German October offensive was taken prisoner and was held in camps at Karlsruhe and Mainz. He survived.

After the war he joined the Chartered Bank of India, Australia and China[1] (today's Standard Chartered) and was sent on the long sea voyage to Bangkok, the capital of Siam (Thailand). He led a fairly active life, enjoying rugby and playing the pipes in a pipe band. He was also a violinist. Like any Scot he was a good dancer and this could well have brought him and mother together. She was a fanatical dancer. (In old age she once told me that, had she not married, she would have been a dancer, despite her diminutive size.) At eighteen she was swept off her feet by thirty year old handsome Billie. Photographs show a very grand, traditional wedding, and they lived happily ever after, despite 'death do us part' an alarming possibility. Both lived to a good age. Mother's last shock must have been waking to find her Billie dead in the bed beside her. She would live on another twenty years. I heard about father's death in a curious way. I was in remotest Skye, camping and climbing with a school party. We were washed out by a deluge and, having retreated to Portree, found the Police had been trying to find me for some days. They told me my father had died so I set off to hitch, bus, train, train, and bus home. Brother Ian from Hong Kong beat me to it, but he had a 48 hours' start. In father's day it would take many weeks to head West-East or vice versa – so they put in *years* in one posting before a long home leave.

Mother, an only child, was born in Bangkok in Siam in May 1904, her father a Scots engineer who was building Siam's railways. One of her memories is of dancing a sword dance, dressed in full Highland dress (Royal Stewart tartan) before the King of Siam, (memories of the musical *The King and I*) and I certainly saw a photo of mother in this rig. I do have a letter from the Secretary of the Bangkok St Andrews Society asking if Mrs Swanson (Gran) would kindly consent to Miss Swanson (mother) giving a Sword Dance performance at the Society's Ball to be held at the Sports Club on 30th January 1920.

When the grandparents retired in the early Thirties they bought a house, 'Caledonia,' in the village of Carrick Castle on Loch Goil, an offshoot of Loch Long, and ran it as a B&B. Sadly Grandfather died in 1939, after the family had sailed for Japan. Ian had been left as a boarder at Dollar Academy. When it appeared there would be the chance to

7

come out to join the family in Japan, Ian was taken out of school, the house sold, and the waiting period was spent in Carrick Castle living with friends.

As a child Mother had several trips 'home' to Scotland, at two years old and five years old (one of her first memories was playing with a toy catamaran in the scuppers of a ship) and later for schooling in Bridge of Allan and Glasgow. Siam was a life of games and parties and beach, with visits to picturesque temples but little social contact locally. She performed in a production of *Yeoman of the Guard*. One journey via the Cape took in the then North and South Rhodesia (Zambia and Zimbabwe). Family legend has it Gran went through the Suez Canal 13 times; quite possible.

I've cuttings from the Siamese newspaper as well as the order of service for the wedding, which was held in Christ Church, Bangkok on the afternoon of 23 February 1926. (A civil ceremony was held at the British Legation in the morning). 'The bride looked singularly sweet, attired in a gown of shimmering iridescent sequins with a long train of pale pink bordered georgette, surmounted with a veil and wreath of orange blossom. She carried a shower bouquet of lilies, roses and white honolulu.' The costumes of the principal bridesmaids, 'two sweet little things,' the Cochrane sisters 'looking after the train, and the bride's mother' are all described in similar style. Father was in kilt with white jacket and all the trimmings. His sister, Nellie Tull, was also present, on holiday from work in Penang. The reception was held on the spacious lawn of the Swanson home in Convent Road, after which they went to the Phya Palace Hotel which they no doubt left dotted with confetti before going on by the Southern Express to Hua Hin for a few days. Everything is thoroughly described, the many presents giving 'an excellent indication of the warmth of feeling for the bride and bridegroom'; something which I'm sure was said of them whenever they had to leave any of their postings in the years ahead.

My parents had a honeymoon and home leave combined, sailing from Bangkok to Singapore on SS *Klang*, then straight on to South Africa, where father's brother Jim ran a chicken farm near Pretoria. They visited the Victoria Falls, Niagara and flowery Madeira. From Dunfermline they toured the north of Scotland and stayed with father's sister in Ireland. Father was then posted to Calcutta in India, squeezing in holiday visits to Darjeeling and Kalimpong. On the next home leave Ian was born in Dunfermline (1930). They toured the Borders, Devon and Ireland again.

This time Colombo would be the posting, for two spells with home leave between. I was born in Colombo in 1934 during the first spell and went home in 1936 with Ian, who then stayed on in Scotland for schooling. Colombo, in retrospect, gave my parents their happiest years, fascinated by ancient civilisations, marvellous beaches, good friends and a reasonable climate. Father took early 16mm ciné film and recorded sites and sights and moments like the first airmail flight arriving. I'm shown being knocked about in the sea's edge before I could walk and swimming would be a lifelong enthusiasm. After that second home leave, in 1939 my parents (and I) travelled to Japan, a country mother commented 'looked so like its unreal depiction in paintings'. Looking back mother wrote that life had been 'sometimes spectacular and always interesting, until the war,' then 'too exciting and tough'.

One sometimes hears criticism of the social life and the 'goings on' of those living and working abroad but this usually the result of the 'doings' of a small minority, something which happens everywhere. Abroad somehow is more 'exotic' and ignorance of the reality is a great producer of exaggeration. If the standard of living may have been higher, with pleasant housing and servants, then there were plenty of drawbacks, like an unhealthy climate, long periods between home leave and children then separated from parents because of health and educational needs. Work itself may not have been congenial, there was a hidebound social life, the snobbery of rank, enervating forced leisure for wives and, in our case, many uncertainties.

My parents were not as stereotyped as most. Golf, to father, was a good walk spoilt; they preferred 'proper' walking, exploring and, above all else, family activities. They were also somewhat unusual in their regard for servants. In the East, everybody, locals and foreigners alike, who had any status, had servants, and let's face it, still do – anywhere. Many thousands of otherwise unemployed people were extremely happy to be servants with the security the employment provided. The system could be exploited (there's nothing good ever that's not twisted for evil) but not very often; it would be self-defeating. (The opposite was not unknown, with servants holding an employer in thrall.) Mother and Father always had servants and treated them honourably, beyond the normal I'm sure. (Home was always a happy place.) On leaving Japan there were gifts and tears from the servants, as there was in South Africa as when the Zulu teenager Ivy, who looked after David, was to lose her 'Ba-ba'. In the 1960s in Scotland we had an unexpected visitor, a man who had been the family cook in Colombo when I was born. He came out of his way to visit us, a visit that thrilled everyone. And look at the letters father received from his Chinese staff at Klang at the end of the war, or his taking one of his Japanese clerks and his family to Tokyo zoo at a time when Europeans were being hassled in the streets by militarised students. Mother simply treated everyone the same, never learned to dissemble, sometimes spoke her mind perhaps too freely,

10

but hers was the shoulder on which many would lay their troubled heads, whether planter's wife or the top politico's spouse. People couldn't resist her genuineness. She had a host of friends. Father was her perfect foil, always calm and strong, loyal to his staff and loyal to the Chartered, at his post among the falling bombs till the last moment. When he escaped his luggage contained nothing personal, but just a suitcase of the bank's most vital records. His quiet strength and courage I came to admire more and more over the years.

With Japan's attacks we were to see another tearing of the thin gauze that separates sense and folly, content and greed, love and hate, peace and war, the impossibility of mankind to keep its heart clean and its hands to itself. Mother would express pity for the poor, often starving people of Japan she saw who, like Everyman, everywhere, wanted little beyond simple needs fulfilled and the hope of seeing the sun rise on the morrow.

Certain threads run through these domestic letters: the family concerns of a new baby, of irrepressible me, of brother and Gran marooned in Scotland, of their social life and friends, of the gathering storm, and I quote sufficiently I hope to give some continuity to these, while using but a part of the extensive material. This is also my story, filling in some of the colours from first hand memory while able to do so. Had I been a couple of years older, how much more I could have recalled.

There is one curiosity in that the (always censored) letters, both to and from Scotland, would only be read many weeks after they were written and posted, the more vital, practical matters being cabled. (Thanks for a birthday parcel might reach the sender four months after the parcel had been dispatched). Watch the dates. In some ways the letters are more diary than letters and I present them as such. One friend felt he was reading a play with its succession of acts. It is the story of very ordinary people and, I hope, thereby may prove interesting and give rare insights for a period which has always had such big drums beating. Ours is a piccolo note; I hope worth playing.

To save a lot of space I have standardised the start and finish of the letters and cut out the endless sloppy greetings. A little of 'Heaps of love, Ian pet, your loving Mummy' goes a long way. The name of the place (address) is given first (in detail the first time), then the day, date, year (sometimes), to whom addressed and by whom written. Mother's letters were naturally addressed to her 'Mummy dearest' but to avoid confusion she is called 'Gran' at the start of letters.

2

The Japanese Baby

Mother wrote some notes for me in later life which remain my only record of movements between Ceylon and Japan:

'Sailed on the P&O *Rajputana* for home in March 1936 (Ian, 5½, missing when you being bathed, thereafter bathed together). Following years in Carrick, Dunfermline, Galway. October 1938 P&O *Ranchi* to Colombo, for six months, in Colombo, Nuwara Eliya, (pronounced: Noo-ray-lee-ya) etc. Peter Wilmshurst best friend. Spring 1939. Same ship to Yokohama. Grandpa Swanson dies. Dad and Mum up Fuji'.

In the early twenty-first century I had a letter out of the blue from a Peter Wilmshurst asking for my date of birth to see if I was by any chance the Hamish Brown who, family tradition had it, was born in the same hospital in Colombo in August 1934, within hours of himself (the Browns and Wilmshursts were good friends). Almost correct; we were in fact born days rather than hours apart. Strange to renew a contact like that.

Japan had remained an ally in World War One but the relationship was less harmonious thereafter. Crown Prince Hirohito however was a guest of George V at Buckingham Palace and the Prince of Wales the following year made a Japanese tour. In 1926 Hirohito became Emperor, a living

God to his people, and for his reign chose the auspicious name *Showa* – Enlightened Peace.

The Thirties saw what was a slow but inexorable slide to war. In 1930 the Japanese military largely seized control of a country in turmoil, in 1931 they took over Manchuria in northern China and scorned Western protests. Japan withdrew from the League of Nations in 1933. Coups and assassinations and political woes were balanced by a surge of industrialization. In 1936 they joined Nazi Germany in a pact and then launched a full-scale invasion of China, with the end of 1937 producing the appalling atrocities of the capital, the 'Rape of Nanking' (prisoners were used for bayonet practice). Alarm bells were ringing as one can glean from mother's letters. Women and children were advised by the Foreign Office to leave Japan – and we, fortunately, did so, father being posted to Klang in Malaya (now Malaysia).

With the outbreak of the Second World War my parents had decided, as Scotland was receiving bombs, that my big brother Ian and Gran (mother's mother) should come out to Japan for safety, all the more desirable when my younger brother was born in Yokohama in December 1940. Ian was taken out of school and the family home, 'Caledonia,' in Carrick Castle in Argyll was sold. Their coming out, however, was not to be. Ian and Gran were stranded in Scotland, and stayed so.

Great friends in Carrick, the McIntyres, offered them a home, one became Aunt Dor and her daughter Margaret was almost a sister to Ian, both going to the local school which never had more than a dozen pupils. Carrick Castle on Loch Goil, a loch running off Loch Long, was reached by the wee steamer *Comet*, sailing from Greenock. Ironically, when we eventually made it back to Scotland, with the war still on and bombs still falling on Scotland, we watched the sky over the hills from Carrick lit up by a raid and, heading to Greenock on the *Comet*, found the gutters were running with syrup from the Tate and Lyle factory.

The topic of Gran and Ian joining us rumbles on through these letters and must have done so through 1939-40 until the time of David's arrival. Only then were the letters home kept. Presumably much of that unrecorded time passed in the usual social round of expat families (monotonously similar everywhere out East) but with a growing unease about the political situation. Writing many years later mother noted, 'My wanderings were a long time ago, mostly before the war, a very different world. We were young then and it was quite a frivolous life, hard work for the men in trying climates, wives unable to do any real work – not allowed to. One had to obtain permission to marry. There was no real security, with a transfer possible at a few weeks warning, or less in an emergency. We played games, swam, walked, danced, had endless parties. Small boys to look after at least meant a real home – but always changing houses, even countries, with the run of hotels and ships and other demands. Fortunately there were always servants, so varied from one country to the next, and so hard to part from'.

This first group of surviving letters was obviously kept as they are all about the arrival of David William Brown, the letters only a daughter could write to her mother and I feel their appearance almost borders on an invasion of privacy yet at the same time what an extraordinary picture they give of a particular time and place, at a period when the greatest world upheaval had begun. Mother was a prolific letter writer, her flow of words hardly able to keep pace with her bursting energy. She kept up an amazing correspondence all her life. I can picture her, back against a tree in Natal, or against a rock on a Tiree beach, knees up like a desk, scribbling by the hour. Letter writing here was one escape from that circumscribed world of being a *memsahib* in the east. So many families only made west of east when they retired. Mother was thirty six when David was born, father a dozen years older, solid, dependable, impish at times, the perfect foil for livewire mother. He is the B in letters, B for Billie. The first letter to have survived is to Ian, my big brother, at home in Scotland.

210 Bluff, Yokohama. 21 November 1940.
To Ian, from Mummy. Thank you very much for your letter. Long before this one reaches you, you will have news of the new baby and I hope won't be at all disappointed if it's a brother! A wee sister would be nice for a change but another boy equally welcome, so we'll see what comes. Maybe by this time you'll have had news of our next destination, if we get a transfer as hoped. Christmas will be over when this gets to you. Sure you would have a nice time, exciting knowing you would be sailing sometime quite soon to join us somewhere, not likely to Japan or China. Queer, writing this, not to know any of these (to us) important, exciting happenings, just waiting for them all and you will likely know everything by cable before this reaches you! Major [dog] is growing quite big... hope you see him sometime soon. If we are moved from here we would take him with us, if to where they allow dogs. Some countries don't so that's another thing for us to 'wait and see,' a lot of big 'ifs' these days.

We have just got a water colour of a sea beach with Fuji in the background. It is a beautifully-shaped mountain and in this autumn weather we get such clear views of it, top covered in snow. The picture will remind us, after leaving, of the real thing and the time we climbed to the top last year. We go a lot of wee walks and visit friends and watch games

16

at the Club and time passes quickly and pleasantly in spite of being anxious to get you beside us and the awful news of all the troubles all over the world, but keep hoping 1941 will see improvements on this year. Hamish getting pink cheeks again. Hot and sunny in middle of day and jolly cold at nights, very like home but not so much rain.

Father always wrote on the other side of mother's letters.

To Ian, from Daddy. Nice cold weather now, cold but bright and sunny. Winter is very nice, not a bit like home. Fuji has a lot of snow already although we have none in Yokohama. Hamish loves drawing Fuji and does it very well. He is such a wild big boy now and loves a rough play with Major. I will put in more stamps. Let me know if you get them. They may not be allowed. Hope you are having a nice time in Carrick.

Almost every letter from father would enclose stamps, the habit continued right through until he retired; all we three boys eagerly awaited these stamps from many countries. Banks often received heavy or registered mail so there were many high value stamps which were treasure-trove for stamp-swapping. The stamps were picked in turn by the three of us and became a good pocket money supplement. But that is looking many years ahead. In the parental letters following, many of the stamp references will be omitted – as will that perennial British interest in the weather.

210 Bluff. 14 December.
To Gran, from Mummy. Again the same address but surely this will be finished in hospital. Sunny frosty weather now. I have walked a lot every morning and yesterday afternoon

17

we had Miss Pocock from the Bank for tea; Billie and she came home together and met the doctor and brought him along as well and we'd a particularly nice tea. Cookie made cream puffs and apple pie and asamaberry pie (like blackcurrant), asparagus sandwiches, bread and butter and ham, so Hamish enjoyed his fancier-than-usual tea. Sugar and flour are the most scarce things to get here but we don't notice much, not taking sugar in tea. These two visitors had just gone and we'd settled down after getting the noisy one off to bed, when a couple Broad came in unexpectedly; nice when folks drop in like that, they are South African and have three children under nine, two nice wee girls Hamish plays with sometimes but doesn't see very much of, because they go to the Convent [School]. They are still here, instead of evacuating like most because he is having a struggle to get money that his father left. Expect they would leave tomorrow if they could get this money out of the country. He has a job as well, of course.

Glad the Club is having a weans' party after all, on 23rd and we'll have the three Broad weans as guests. Only a dozen white weans left. The youngest Broad is a wee boy of 2½ who thinks Hamish is just the stuff, he is a bright wee thing and Hamish really plays nicely and gently with him although he can be so blooming rough and tough with big ones.

15 December. Very early next morning Mummie dearest and no sleep this night, as wee B isn't being so very late with the December date. Went to bed as usual and Billie phoned doctor at 3.30. I wasn't terribly sure but didn't want to waste time, have had so many collie-wobbles with the kicking and wind, so sure enough it's actually on its way now at last and it's now 6.30 and I'm in hospital all set, pains coming and going, bathed and all fixed and, as usual these days, just waiting. The doctor drove me along just after four so hope your cable will go off later today, precious one.

Yokohama General Hospital 17 December 1940.
To Gran, from Mummy. Dearest, it's terribly hard to believe that 'David William' is only two days old, he looks so nice to be so young, the other two were queer looking at that age in comparison. Today is the first time he has been all dressed up, in a fancy cotton long dress you made for Ian and an adorable wee jersey. He doesn't look silly the way the other two did in fancy sort of clothes and it's hard to realise he's heavier than they were at birth. He is so neat but has much fuller cheeks, is such a nice colour and so smooth and well finished, not that either of the other were anything but. Hamish was big and thin and had lines on face and not such a good colour to begin with, although after a few weeks he really was a beauty, he filled out so suddenly and quickly. Ian was messed-about to begin with, with food nonsense, etc and it took him some months to become the good-looking fellow he has stayed – not half swanking, am I? But really, they are fine healthy specimens if, as we often tell Hamish, they would behave as well as they look! This one is unbelievably good. He roared and roared and roared when he was newly born, long before they got him away from me. It was a relief to hear such a fine pair of lungs, there certainly couldn't be much wrong with a baby who could make so much noise.

I didn't mind that it was another boy for us, really expected that, but I was so rude to the doctor about the stitches, just wouldn't stop talking, especially giving him a row about stitches shouldn't be necessary – as if the poor man could help that, and I could never be so cheeky to anyone normally but the whiff of chloroform was a help and though quite conscious during the birth (more so than

19

when Ian was born even) they had to put me right under to get the stitches in, as I just wouldn't 'relax' as told to. He arrived sooner than they expected, at the last minute, again because it was 'dry,' they seemed surprised that it was such a big baby when I'd been so neat (as most people thought, but I felt I'd a good hefty barrel being carried about). As usual, the hard bulge all baby and no padding. David William arrived at 12 and the pains were every five minutes right from the beginning, even in the house, but of course, getting stronger and longer all the time and then quicker. I was calling 'Billie, Ian, Mummie' constantly, when more than half conscious and that everything was 'all right,' not only about the baby being a boy, or the stitches, but about the war and everything, that it was going to be 'all right,' so that's a good omen I feel. Have felt all the waiting time that the new baby wasn't being affected at all by all the worry and the troubled times; it seemed to be absolutely apart from everything else. He sleeps all the time and yet has made a splendid effort at feeding, knows what to do all right and we both seem to be just perfectly fit; am sure I'll nurse him all right. My first really sane and awake words after the chloroform were, 'Poor Hamish, I never mentioned him'. He arrived much more easily than his brothers. Really was very excited, more so than either time before. So good to have the wee one safely here, as I felt so personally responsible for it and sometimes worried about it maybe not being a sensible time to enlarge the family.

Even on Saturday before beginning your mail, I'd been shopping and walked a lot and at *tiffin* time Billie brought Chisholm in for a drink and we promised to have dinner with him in the hotel on Sunday unless (as it turned out) I was otherwise engaged! I've often thought a girl was too much to wish for, so really fully expected a boy; it seemed too easy to get all we wanted in the family line, each time we have deliberately chosen to have a baby. No wonder births aren't easy, we should pay sweetly for these precious wee goats, the bad bit is so quickly over and forgotten and they are worth everything. Can scarcely believe we have such a nice big family – Billie laughs at me being so proud of them but he really is much more so – he is pricelessly proud of David being such a walloper; 8 lbs indeed! On Sunday, Billie was in here seeing me at 11 o'clock, on his way to meet Hamish from Sunday school, then in again at 2.30 and then back with Hamish and roses at 5 o'clock, so a busy, exciting day.

This place, Yokohama General Hospital, is perfectly run and allows nuns. They certainly do everything they do terribly well. The maternity wing is so attractive, with lovely sunny rooms, everything in very good taste and delicious food and plenty of it. The Sisters are dears, very cheery and nice, then we each have a private nurse, engaged and recommended by the doctor. Ours is Japanese and she knows about two words of English and I know about three words of Japanese. But she is young and pleasant and willing, so it's all right with the Sisters supervising everything. She sleeps in the baby's room at night and is entirely ours. She is kept quite busy, as you know it's always one or the other's feeding time, bath, temperature, weight, bed, flowers etc, really a lot to do although no 'worry' about food, that's hospital responsibility.

Certainly couldn't be more comfy and even if slightly disappointed that Ian and you aren't here for the arrival, it's very good for me not to be evacuated and away from B, and then the glorious hope of a transfer, that would likely let us all get together in a few more months. I've been quite busy writing thanking notes, it's amazing the folks who send flowers, people we don't know very well as well as real pals, and in spite of so many people away. Billie and Hamish

21

come in on way to office and school, then at *tiffin* time and then in the evening, so the time simply flies. Hamish is very thrilled with the baby. How do you like the name? We only suddenly decided about it yesterday.

Hospital, 18 December.
To Gran, from Mummy. I'm so thrilled I don't know where to begin. Young David certainly has brought good news behind him, can hardly believe it all yet, it's queer how so many good or bad things come all at one time and how the bad bits in this case have turned out very lucky. If Billie hadn't had that queer upset (not like a definite illness) we would never have got a transfer. This baby too, if he hadn't been on the way, we might have felt it necessary to take Hamish to definite safety and look what a nuisance some of us being in Australia or Canada would have been. It all seems very wonderful, the way it's 'panned out,' as Daddy used to say. Sorry you have had so much work and trouble and writing to do with the house, also passages and permits etc. but once the house was fixed and you got our posting cable you would surely have a good breather. We are hoping you would live with Dorothy and stay in Carrick.

After writing yesterday Billie brought your welcome letters at *tiffin* time, then the cable in the evening. This *tiffin* time came our transfer news: Singapore for orders which might mean anywhere in the Straits Settlements. David has made this a historic week for our family, hasn't he? Hamish was at a party in school yesterday and has three next week, so he is nicely fixed for Xmas and then we'll have a New Year, Christening, farewell party, all in one. What relieved feelings we all have.

Yokohama Hospital, 17 December.
To Ian from Mummy. I wish you could see your wee-est

22

brother, if you could you would not be at all sorry that 'it' isn't a sister. When Hamish heard the news on Sunday at lunch time he said 'I wish it was a sister' but when he saw him after tea, he was simply delighted and has never mentioned being sorry again and just loves looking and looking at him umpteen times every day. He often says to Daddy 'Kiss Mummy and come and see the baby now.' Have lots of lovely flowers from friends and they look beautiful in this pretty peach colour and green room. Thanks for your two letters written two months ago. Glad you are liking school; you seem to be very good at knitting, very useful these days. How do you like the baby's name? We are so pleased with him and hope you will see him before he is many months old.

19 December.
To Ian, from Mummy. Just a wee scrap added before posting. Your wee-est brother is progressing splendidly. This has been an exciting week for us, really quite a historic one for our family, so many nice things coming all at one time: young David first, then the cable from Gran, then the next day, the cable from Head Office with the transfer news which is splendid and you will be getting our cable about that now. So hasn't it all worked out well after all, your postponed passages, the work and worry of getting the house sold (successfully in the end)? If it hadn't been for David being on the way, they (British Consul, Daddy, Bank) might have bullied me into taking Hamish to Australia!

David sleeps all the time and feeds so well and looks so placid and contented, it shows a baby isn't affected by the troubled time it's born in, if the parents are well and happy, even if worried, beforehand. Don't know our exact destination but anywhere in the Straits will be ok – all fairly hot, like Colombo but Hamish will go to a school up-country in the hills (like Nuwara Eliya in Ceylon). Much handier than India, India is so huge and has such long journeys. Daddy will like working with Malays and Chinese, and a nice change, seeing we were in India before. Wonder if round Africa will be your best way out to join us.

Yokohama General Hospital. 20 December.
To Gran, from Mummy. Your mail only being posted today and here goes already our next week's one but expect I have more time now than next week. Poor wee David had his tail cut this morning but fed as well as ever. He is the sleepiest, plumpest, most placid baby imaginable; there are two other babies who cry a good deal. Yesterday and day before I was dashed sore with the milk coming but it has settled down beautifully; the Sister's massaging was a big help. Sykes was in last night, the first visitor, Billie and Hamish three times every day. Hamish finishes school today; glad it's the weekend, for B to keep an eye on him! Then his parties next week will keep him busy and after that we (nurse, baby and I) will soon be home. The other two babies are both German, one born just the night before David and the other on Sunday night. Neither had our American doctor of course but the Sisters had a busy weekend.

Such a spate of lovely flowers today, I'm almost ashamed to have so many in one room. Lovely scent of roses, pots of cyclamen and begonias, a flat dish with tree, etc, worked into a scene, what the Japs excel in, these miniature 'gardens' [more on this later]. Hard to believe baby David is only five days old now, with tail all tidy; and nicely into the way of feeding, each day flies past. Have just had a visit from our *amah-san*, with flowers. Had such a topping letter from Beatrice in Canada. With Ian and you out beside us, it would be quite a good idea to spend our next leave in Canada, if money could be arranged, if we get leave before the war is over, that is. Have lots of thanking notes to write.

23 December

Eight day old David thriving. Doctor delighted with me; he suggested the other day that I could go home for Xmas but nine days seemed a bit risky and we'll wait until eleven days. He thought I'd be disappointed not being at home then but too delighted with everything to worry about Xmas, especially as the stitches only came out yesterday and I haven't been up much yet – got on a chair for half an hour today. As well as the huge meals, they are now giving me milk or ovaltine after every feed.

Hamish came in with B on his way to office this morning. On holiday now and he had the dog with him and was going home and then out shopping with Ichisan and has a party this afternoon. Having cold frosty sunny weather and they both came in glowing with health, Hamish in kilt and jersey. He'll get silk shirt on in afternoon and new tie. We'll be sorry to leave this fine cold climate but other things much more important these days. They went to Tokyo Zoo yesterday, (we've been talking about it since before last Xmas) with a man in the office and his son, same size Ham. Japanese and Scots families had a good day, very exciting for the boys. Billie came in before and after Church. He went because there was a musical stunt extra.

Hamish brought me some Japanese wee model things they use in the plant 'gardens'. He bought them on the street: small houses, bridges etc. Giving Dorys Moffat a bowl etc with goldfish for Xmas. They have been transferred to Kobe and are taking their furniture etc with them. Rotten luck, newly married, buying furniture and getting such an appalling transfer. If it had been out of the country they'd not be caring about furniture. They were both in seeing me yesterday, so was Ichisan and then later Mr and Mrs Fox came with Billie, on Saturday Norma McVittie and Mrs

25

Mendleson in afternoon, and Mrs Hudgell (she has baby one month old) in morning, so less spare time than ever.

Later same day Mummie precious and a mail came from you today, dated 1st October, one written just after Jessie had been with you. Ever so many thanks for it, how you managed to write so much between the worries of house and passages. Lots of pals have had good bargains of your nice things, but then it's always a little more £.s.d. separate from house and hope some day we can make it all up to you. Just after scrawling to you this morning, I had visitors: Mrs Broad and an English girl married to a German, then Hamish, then Billie and Jones, so they went home together, complete with my umbrella that Hamish brought, also Major. I was up and didn't feel wobbly at all, just a bit pins and needles in feet.

27 December
We came home yesterday in nice time for tea and the lad's six o'clock feed. He got dressed up in one of his best frocks, lace bib on top of shawl, lace bonnet and he just tore at the ribbons, he was furious. He loved his first big bath. I really was glad to get to bed and have stayed in it all day except for paris; dressing in winter is such a plister. We're a comfy house with the steam heating. Have written three dozen cards home, will do the Eastern ones later. Baby feeding well, mostly from me and a little powdered milk (Canadian) each time. A mixture like this makes weaning so easy.

'Paris' in the last paragraph may puzzle. It was the family euphemism for going to the loo. I have no idea why the French capital (if it is) was so denigrated. To have a pee was given the puzzling if onomatopoeic 'shi-shi,' and only very recently, and quite by chance, I learned *shii-shii-swa* was the Japanese for urinating. In earlier letters the reference to David's 'tail' presumably was to his 'shi-shi thing'. Recently, the weird topic of family euphemisms for bodily functions was cheerfully discussed at a local Rotary evening meal which shows how things have changed since Japan in 1940.

Something I recall very clearly was the large, flat, oval, blue dish (about 1½ inches deep) which held the miniature 'Japanese gardens' which is mentioned twice in this letter. It eventually came to Scotland and when it was broken (I can't recall how) mother actually burst into tears. It was treasured by all of us. Sand, gravel, stones, twigs, flowers, greenery of a *bonsai* character was built up in the dish to make a landscape in which stood a miniature Fuji, three houses, a temple and a *torii* gateway, an arched bridge (spanning a silver-paper stream) and with a fisherman wearing a wide straw hat poling his boat on a lake of mirror glass. I thought it magical – and was surprised, reading this letter seventy years on, to note that I'd bought some of the miniatures. Those that survived are now in the Museum of Childhood in Edinburgh.

210 Bluff 27 December 1940.
To Ian from Mummy. Here we are home again but young David hated being all dressed up to come home and certainly knew there was a change of bed and everything, because he cried far more than he has ever done before. Major was frightened and barked when he first heard him. Hamish says he sounded just like lots of cats mewing and he's about right. Hope you and Gran have addressed your letters to us lately c/o the Bank in Singapore, because letters take ages. Via Canada or America is quicker, but it won't matter much knowing that you will soon be coming [one of the letters home had the envelope marked 'via Siberia'].

Wonder what you were doing at Xmas; we were thinking

27

Amah Itchisan, Hamish, Nurse Tanaka-san, and baby David. Note frost protection on the bush behind.

about you, always are. Daddy and Hamish were at a Xmas *tiffin* party in Sykes and on Monday Ham was at a party in the Club; 60 children there, all nationalities. Most of Hamish's real friends are away now. They had a good time, Santa Claus came, and there was a big tree, and lots of games. Broads had a fine party on Tuesday, so your big wee brother had a good Xmas and has lots of nice presents, mostly small things like books and crayons, puzzle games, things to make. Our own Xmas tree is still on the dining table, first there at breakfast on Xmas morning as the house is all decorated.

To Ian, from Daddy. I took Hamish up to the Zoo in Tokyo on Sunday and he was very thrilled to see all the animals. It is a big zoo with nearly all the well-known animals. He was very funny with the Sea Lions. A man was selling fish to give them but he did not wait for money just climbed the barrier and grabbed a fish. He did not even take off his woollen gloves so they have a nasty fishy smell and had to be washed. One of our Japanese clerks and his little boy went with us and the two small boys had a good time. Hamish liked the monkeys too and has been trying to imitate them on our trees in the garden.

Mummie and baby David are home now and both very well.

1 January 1941.

To Gran from Mummy. Wonder if you began posting letters to us in Singapore directly you got the news before Xmas. Letters take ages to get there from home, much worse than coming here. It seemed such a shame that, just as soon as you had the house and everything sold and packing done, you got the word to postpone. But then you would be relieved like we were, when our transfer came through, as it solved the evacuation problem. If Billie hadn't been sick and we had no transfer it would have been terribly difficult to know what to do; they might have bullied me into taking the weans away; there are scarcely any American or British children left here, the majority of the women who are still here, have no weans or big ones parked in schools in Canada etc. Could easily have meant Australia for us and that would have meant a change of plans for Ian and you. A good thing you weren't stuck in Canada. [The reason why Ian and Gran were now not to join us only became known to us after the war. I describe something of the story at the end of this chapter.] It all turned out well because now we

29

can meet in a British place, even if terribly hot. Oh, this lovely cold climate; we came here ten years too late.

Expect to sail from Kobe and think we'll go there by boat – a big Maru one due to sail on 30th January (British ships can't say ahead when sailing) and Singapore have been asking when we're coming. This one on the second of February is definite and a good new American President Line ship, each cabin with its own bathroom and paris so should be comfy, fast too, due to arrive Singapore on 14th – calling at Shanghai, Hong Kong and Manila.

Home a week now and have been very lazy and careful. Young Davie asleep in pram in garden in the sun at the moment. A quiet New Year was very acceptable. Have the decorations up still as this is the big holiday. Xmas only gives offices etc. the one day but now they have three days and although it's Bank Balance it's not so fierce as in most places.

David loves his bath and has an admiring audience every morning. The wee nurse is very capable and nice and quite strict, she and Hamish enjoy going out together and she knits for Davie in her spare time and loves doing it. I only wish it were more necessary, he has far more than enough woollies. I clear out of our room after having breakfast in bed, play with Hamish then watch the bath, etc., then the room is clean and tidy and ready for me to get back to bunk for his ten o'clock feed. Taking special milk (supposed to be creamier than the usual) four times a day and invalid port once a day. I have actually taken neat cod liver oil, also liver, so it's wonderful what our infant will make one do. Only have the one precious bottle of port, good brand, saved for this, took it over from our predecessor Marrables when we came here.

Again posting a pile of cards. Think that's the Eastern ones about finished – only to people we know well. Lots of good friends all over the Straits, so don't mind where we're sent. Will be living a very quiet life wherever it is. Singapore would be expensive and too big so rather hope it isn't there. Country ones would be nearer the hills for school. As long as we all get together.

Davie lad isn't 3 weeks old yet. Not sure of exact weight, as scales (on loan from McVittie) are in grams and that's muddling. Hamish loves watching all his performances. He is looking so well, don't know how he isn't as skinny as a needle, because his energy and nonsense is unbelievable. It's high time he had his big brother's kilt, as his wee frill is getting far too short. Nurse and baby are in Hamish's old room, it is quieter and both bedrooms have lovely windows with heavenly views of Fuji. Hamish trots off to bed upstairs and has never once objected to his change of beds; he is good in some ways, not afraid of dark or anything. This would have been an ideal house for you and Ian to join us in. Queer being back to normal shape again, flat tummy, finding and using a belt Jessie brought out to me in Colombo.

Would you please keep my first letter from hospital; some day I would like to compare it to first one from home to B when Ian was born, I know it's in the bottom of a trunk.

Wonder if you are still in 'Caledonia' or somewhere else in Carrick. In some ways so sorry to think of house sold but some day might hope to have a smaller one in Carrick; the place itself is ideal.

21 January 1941.
To Gran from Mummy. Perhaps Iza spent Xmas with you but afraid she wouldn't be able to if she's Polish Officers to look after in the Dunfermline house. Changed days since Ian's arrival there, nearly eleven years ago; remember Iza being horrified at the suggestion of letting the house in

31

summertime. All troubles and hard-upness really seems quite good for us all, we can see things more sensibly. So glad you two keep so fit and hope the Xmas money would help pay for extras like clothes, etc. you bought for Ian. David's vaccination didn't hurt at all. He is beginning to smile and looks so bright when awake with big blue grey eyes (as if he could have any other sort of eyes in this family!)

Most of our packing is finished: wanted to do it early and be free the last week to let me have time to practise handling young Davie, along with last minute parties. We are having a cocktail party on Saturday and hope to have the lad christened that afternoon and photos taken. Sykes is having a party on Wed night before we go. We all had tea at Club on Sunday, I went in taxi. Hamish had a fine play with the nice Danish girl and the two families had tea together. Packing has been done in such short snatches. Got all the quaint plates etc packed in unwanted clothes in big trunks, as there wasn't enough china to get a packer in (nothing valuable, just amusing dishes we likely couldn't get elsewhere). The boat-shaped flower dish heavy but unusual and nice that made quite difficult packing. [I inherited this beautiful object] Now we hope to only have suitcases in cabin. Hamish is wearing a 13 shoe so if you bring any sandals out for him, they'd better be size 1. Margaret's letter was very good, almost the same words as Ian's but much better written. Poor lamb [Ian] having to write so regularly when he'd rather be doing sums.

It's now 7 o'clock on morning of 23rd of January and a week today we sail. Meant to finish off mail after tea yesterday but the padre came in to arrange about the wee lad's christening. We arranged 3.30 on Saturday as he'll be fed and happy then. It suddenly gets much colder about five and he would be furious at that time, getting hungry. We'll try and have photos taken, then after the service we'll have a small tea-fight, just the necessary Godfathers and one God-mother, who will have been in Church with us. All these Godparents seem such a plister to us but English Church demands them! Sykes will be one and the man Brown. We think he came to Kobe late last night so we haven't seen him yet. He is going to live with Sykes meantime, then take over from us here. Hoped to see McVitties last night to ask her to be Godmother, she's easily my best friend left. Then quite a big cocktail party at night, to really celebrate. Some of the few remaining women have had notices advising them much more strongly than before to leave and even some men who aren't tied with businesses.

We had dinner at the Club last night and saw a good film, Sonia Henie in a lovely skating show. Met lots of pals, the only time and place there is ever a big gathering of white people these days. Posting what will be your second last letter from Japan. We're jolly sorry in some ways to be leaving but, oh, the poor local people, their food is getting so scarce and bad. There is no anti-British feeling with them, just the few idiots in power making all the trouble and the military the real big nuisance. Have met such nice folks too and been very happy and comfy here in spite of home affairs lately. Had a letter from Percy Wicks in Singapore (he used to be in Colombo). Billie wrote to him, to find out about taking the dog but definitely not, utterly impossible. He has no idea where we are being sent, thinks B has to get an official letter about that, in Hong Kong. Very little of our news; the main news is heart-breaking in some ways. [The Blitz, U-boat activity, Malta under attack, the *Ark Royal* sunk etc.] Everything should be all right eventually.

210 Bluff, Yokohama. 26 January 1941.
To Gran, from Mummy. Well David has got his first big

Proud parents with David, 15th December 1940.

day over, very successfully. Only wish you and Ian had been with us but couldn't risk leaving his christening until we all got together. It seemed a job to get over as soon as possible because of the move. All ready to go now, our big party over, a jolly good combined celebration for David, farewell, welcome to the new man, especially having had no party of our own at Xmas. Not so tiring or exciting as I expected. Photographer came. He took photos of baby alone, and along with Hamish, and all four of us together. [These survived.] Also took snaps in garden just after that, a borrowed camera but too cold not to have baby well wrapped up.

All this was quite a hustle after D's two o'clock food, then to Church for 3.30 in taxi, Hamish well warned to behave and actually he was very good all day. During the ceremony he said, "Are these people coming home with us for tea?" otherwise kept quiet. We were all standing round the font, Sykes and Brown Godfathers, Mrs McVittie Godmother, her husband, also Mrs Dixon. The padre held the baby so nicely and rocked him in his arms (like Grandpa did at Ian's Christening) when he cried but no wonder he objected, he got three quite big handfuls of water sprinkled on his head. It wasn't a long service and it really seemed better in Church than in house as we first thought. The padre gave David a book of child's prayers with attractive pictures in it. When Hamish had had a good look at it later on he said "It's cute" so we all laughed. Nice young, quite cheery padre. A big tea party. Had heaps of different sandwiches, apple, cherry and asamaberry pies, cream puffs and sponge cakes and biscuits, strawberries to finish up with (the first this year); a very nice tea. Nine of us made quite a party. They all thought Hamish would be sick, he ate so much. Let down his kilt again, it was scandalously short but looks fine now – definitely the last time it can be fixed. [I've just recalled that in one of my *mots* recorded by mother I asked her something about "a vest and thunderpants".]

Some left at six, others stayed on and the first arrival for cocktail party was very early. Luckily a bottle feed for David, then some scramble getting myself changed – but it all fitted in beautifully, the nurse still with us, makes it all so comfy, fixing the wee lad, his clothes, baths, meals etc. When we came back he was well and truly admired, had his orange juice and some water, then a lovely sound sleep! McVitties sent him a lovely silver pusher and spoon. Had nice white tulips in vases in sitting room and pink sweet-peas on dining table, also plum blossom with fir in bowls. The house looked perfectly nice although our own odds and ends are packed. Just two photos of Ian still on mantelpiece. Billie roped and locked three trunks and camphor-wood box the other day, so our heavy luggage is ready very early. It goes with us, seeing we are going by ship.

Everything went smoothly at the cocktail party; two boys from Club came to help and Cookie made good eats and the no 1 *amah*, Ichisan was splendid, must have been nearly fifty people, as we invited over forty and asked others when we met them. From about 8.30 onwards the piano was going strong and singing full blast. Sykes played but Chisholm played more, catchy, well-known songs; then at 10 we had tea and I hoofed it to feed the wean, tea was a nice change and a cold impromptu meal – didn't expect to have guests at 10 from a 6.30 invitation, but it was fun and they all enjoyed it and had sandwiches and pies left from tea, also cold pheasant and salad and plenty potato salad and crab – absolutely pot-luck, which went down so well, unexpected parties seem so good and we had purposely made extra sandwiches in afternoon. Ichisan is very good at preparing beforehand and her own attractive Japanese clothes look lovely. I like that about this place, the women servants looking so nice, so superior and quiet and pleasant. Both wee lads slept without once waking up through the noise, a fine party and very cheery for these days!

Kobe, Japan, 2 February 1941.
It seems a long time since this letter was begun and it will be the last from Japan. A relief to have the first lap of our journey over, very comfy but oh, thank goodness we packed most things early as there were parties to go out to and people popping in all the time, bathing and feeding David and so much small packing that couldn't be done before-hand and planning where things had to go, for so many stages of the journey. Get so dashed attached to the place and people and sorry to leave in many ways. However, now the biggest strain is over – the actual leaving. One of the worst bits was the dog having to be left. Excitement too of going during these queer, troubled times and feeling so lucky, going together and realising what a difference that makes, our separations bad enough before. I hate to think of what it would have been like, leaving B here, to maybe be interned. Surely not; you'd think they'd get away on any ship that would be sent to take the Diplomatic people away (if trouble actually comes and we still hope it won't, but they seem to have gone too far to escape being drawn into the mess – so a lot think); there is absolutely no anti-British feeling to be noticed, rather the opposite, they definitely don't like the Germans, although so many are here. Afraid Dorys Moffat will even be forced to go. We suggested her coming to Singapore with us as there seems nothing to go to Australia for, no relations or friends. She hasn't been here long enough to know people at all, so few women in the place now. They at once went to the Consul and found out that it was quite impossible, she would get in with a husband going to work there but definitely not with anyone

else, even as a nurse, governess or anything. We were afraid it would be like that. Hong Kong is bad in that way, even wives aren't allowed in there now. A nice young couple left Yokohama very bucked at husband's transfer and she had to take the first ship away to Canada as her home is there. We won't feel really comfy until you two join us but that seems reasonable enough to hope for, close relations are entirely different.

Hope before this reaches you, you will know how things stand about permission to enter Malaya. Don't be worried if there is a big gap in letters now, as they will take ages from the Straits and even ones posted in Shanghai and Hong Kong won't be quick. Maybe by that time you won't be reading letters; would like to think you'd be on your way. But it may take time to fix things up. Will send as little money as possible home; better for you to use what you have and keep a note of what we owe you. It would be impossible for you to bring much out of the country. Hope to much more than square when we get together. The permit to send from here was cut down to next to nothing so there hasn't been time for much to accumulate in London. Insurances and passages, anything needed now, would have to come from this end, which will be possible from a British place but hopeless from Japan. What a lot of money complications the war has caused, as well as all the more dreadful things and being a banker doesn't help much although they understand things more easily.

Young Davie is not minding the change at all so he should be a good traveller. Don't know what news I've written, seem to have been to far more parties than expected but Yokohama Sykes had a big cocktail party, then dinner on our last night, not such a hilarious night as our party but a lovely meal twelve of us and only two women. How cheery people keep; really wonderful.

On Sunday we went to Club for last time for *tiffin* and tea, watched games and Major and Hamish had a good time with pals, then out to dinner, Monday night a party in Spicer's – all these men grass-widowers, wives and families in Canada or Australia. Seems free and easy here and more home-like than other places. Our staff so sorry, the nurse and Ichisan always counting the days, really crazy about the weans and spoil the boys especially. They produced parcels at last minute, so did several friends, instead of flowers, had some lovely plants sent on board: a big basket of lovely tulips as well. The whole staff came on board, all beautifully turned out, even old Cookie, the women in lovely kimonos, beautiful cloth that couldn't be bought now. Lovely big *Asama Maru*. We had two huge cabins and bathroom and passage, so private and comfy, a suite really. Two office men came on board too, they are much more like ourselves than any B has ever worked with, we can be much more friendly and equal with these locals. They do have a far higher standard of living than our usual office staff. Sykes awfully sorry to see us go and yet relieved as well. A shame he can't see his baby when it's younger – she arrived on Sunday, a week earlier than expected. We were sorry to go and glad when we actually sailed, some of the strain over. Comfy ship and delicious food, very rough seas that night but weans absolutely ok – lovely working with the baby and now are having such a nice break in Kobe, being thoroughly spoiled in Hare's house, another Chartered grass-widower, he's accountant here and has lovely big bank house. Hope to sail from here soon now, expect to go on President ship this afternoon. Scramble to get letters off.

The envelope of this last letter from Japan survives, postmarked Kobe, 3.2.41. It was addressed to Master Ian Brown, c/o Swanson at Carrick Castle, marked *Via*

America and was opened by the censor on reaching Britain. There are a couple of earlier envelopes as well, the only one not censored being addressed to Master Ian Brown, Parkfield, Dollar (school boarding house, before thoughts of joining parents). It is marked *Via Siberia*. The franking on two others (both opened for an examiner) is illegible, both were for Grannie Swanson at Caledonia, Carrick, and marked *Via America*, one 'per *Empress of Asia*' (which would end up a burnt-out wreck in the sea off Singapore in 1942). The stamp designs show views of Fuji, the famous arch and a temple at Nikko, and flowers, the Japanese emblem being the chrysanthemum.

The programme of taking evacuee children overseas was stopped in October 1940 following the horrific sinking of the *City of Benares* by a Nazi submarine. 77 children (out of 100) died in the explosion or in the sea or of exposure in flooded lifeboats. 19 such sailings had been made: 11 to Canada, 3 to Australia, 3 to New Zealand, 2 to South Africa. 16 arrived safely; one was torpedoed without loss of life and one returned to port immediately on hearing of the *Benares* sinking. There was never any consistent planning at home, or in the East. Many wives and children were evacuated from Hong Kong but most went to the Philippines only to be interned there. In the case of Malaya Churchill twice suggested evacuating women and children but both the civil and military heads rejected any such idea. Before 1941 ended 1500 mothers and children left anyway.

3

A Boy's Recollections

Retrieving childhood memories is a challenge yet there are images, sharp and clear, which seem to lie too deep to be other than authentic. They are little things on the whole, the little things of a child's world of discovery.

Of Yokohama I remember nothing beyond our house and garden up on the Bluff, then, and still (the Yamate area), an upmarket suburb with many 19th century houses for foreign workers like father. Yokohama was one of the early treaty ports so there was a long history of foreign input. Both Tokyo (today reaching south almost to Yokohama) and Yokohama were largely destroyed in the Great Kanto Earthquake of 1923 when 100,000 people lost their lives. Today's Tokyo would be unimaginable.

A memory which cannot be retrospectively gained was my becoming very interested in the mountain Fujiyama, that graceful symbol of the country, which was visible from our house.[2] On one occasion, I recall I sat on the window seat and cried, firstly because my parents had gone off to climb Fuji without taking me and, secondly, because I could not see them on its slopes – hardly surprising as the mountain was thirty miles away! Fuji went into the background of all my early drawings I'm told – not quite in the style of Hokusai or Hiroshige! There were times, decades on, when I was discovering the Alps, when my parents slapped me down with a 'When you've climbed as high as we have...' Fuji is 12,388 ft (3,776m). There's a gentle satisfaction in being able to blame them for my later lifetime of hills and mountains. They were first of all walkers, country-goers, simply enjoying the lure of landscape; upwards was simply a natural progression which I would take to a greater height so to speak. My birthright was the outdoors, with them and then, like a fledgling bird, set free. Fuji for my parents was just a two day September (1939) trudge up a path among the cinders of the volcano. On top they looked down on a crater of reddish brown with dirty white streaks of snow. I was consoled with their declaration that Fuji in the view was better than Fuji underfoot.

Fuji is normally ascended in two days with July and August the busy season so mother and father waited for a quieter September climb. Like any summit of such height, altitude sickness can occur, and dehydration, and the summit could be freezing no matter what the temperature below. Those with energy enough can circuit the crater rim in an hour. Pilgrims were given, or bought, long, thick, ceremonial, walking poles to help them up the cinder paths. I can remember these but I doubt if the parental sticks left Japan. Ironically, they climbed Fuji on 3 September 1939, the day war was declared with Germany. Fuji must have made a deep impression for many letters home from my school in South Africa had drawings of Fuji, the spelling at times somewhat errant – like 'Fujeamer.'

Gardens have always been prominent in my life. Children played outdoors all the time then, particularly those of us living in countries with a more generous ration of sun. Japan's is the first garden I recall, with its distinctive Japanese style of well-placed pond, and a sculpted lantern and temple in stone. The grass I recall as being coarse to

Mother and Hamish in the Yokohama Garden, 1941.

touch and a line of trees enclosed all. The oddest thing was how, in winter, small trees or shrubs were protected from the frost by having their branches wrapped in straw, creating strange sculptural shapes. Several photos show us posing in front of these. In some photos I hold the dog, Major, an Airedale, a breed I know my parents had in

Ceylon when I was born there in 1934. In one snap I pose with a teddy bear and other toys against a snowy background. Beside the commercial Christening photographs (which came out perfectly well) there are many snaps of family. David appears in the arms of the nurse Tanaka-san, and I pose with Ichisan, the boss *amah*. There is one of me holding hands with two Japanese tots, another in a crowd my age gazing at a puppet show. I pose in Japanese dress for a birthday photo in the garden and several photos show the remembered moon-like, paper parasols. It was exotic but not seen then as such. Small boys accept where they are as being normal, a simplicity of being which we can never return to. Childhood amnesia airbrushes both good and bad from our memories. The Japanese adored children, boys especially, and I could have been thoroughly spoilt but my parents tempered any indulgence. Nobody would dream of hitting a child.

In many of the garden photographs I am clad in Fair Isle jersey and kilt. The tartan is forgotten but later we all sported the Macmillan tartan from mother's side of the family, the 'ancient Macmillan' for we would not have been seen dead in the garish yellow of the 'dress Macmillan'. There was no doubt about our Scottishness. I was James Macmillan on my birth certificate but always called Hamish. Father and all but one of his brothers and sisters followed the national trait of dispersal, the diaspora that saw Scots scatter across the globe. In a couple of years that would lead to a strange gathering of the Browns in Durban.

We sometimes went off to stay at the seaside (Akya Beach?) where we would always pick up interesting shells on the sands – the start of a lifelong activity! Not far along the coast was a residence of the Emperor Hirohito. Before one of his visits officials would come to ask us, most politely, if we had any beautiful shells from the beach and, if so, could we part with them so they could be returned to the sands to give the divine Emperor the pleasure of finding them. How Japanese! The Emperor, though we did not know it then, was an internationally-renowned conchologist and I'm sure would have found our pickings less than exciting. Days later we probably collected the same shells again. Did the Emperor ever walk those sands again? In 1946 he renounced his divinity and many then regarded him as a war criminal.

These dish-miniatures of temple (*otera*), arch (*torii*), bridge (*hashi*) were no doubt a result of our family visit to the thousand year old sacred site of Nikko, today a World Heritage Site, sacred to both Buddhist and Shinto faiths. In the latter part of the nineteenth century wealthy traders and others retreated there rather as the Indian bureaucracy headed to the cool heights of Simla. I can remember some of what I saw and my reactions of awe: the magnificent trees, endless steps, the arched bridge at the start, a many tiered pagoda, the shrines and temples with tiled roofs with curly corners, with huge scary 'golden' figures, red-lacquered pillars and demoniac paintings. (My Fuji drawings often had these as foreground.) I brought back a brass image of the three monkeys with hands over ears, eyes and mouths – to hear no evil, see no evil, speak no evil. They came back to Scotland. So did a pack of *round* playing cards, which were only ever used on special occasions.

And so did a toy I've not seen since, what looked like a brick-sized wooden block, but which pulled apart into a table, chairs, stools and footrests, forming a sort of 3D jigsaw puzzle, a great deal harder to reassemble than to prise apart. The table bore the red 'sun' symbol of Japan, which had long faded with wear and tear over the years.

Most dramatic of memories were small folded objects of paper which, when dropped into a bowl of water, slowly unfolded (like a time-lapse film) to grow into graceful water lilies. Magic. Marvellous. I've seen poor imitations of something similar but the exquisite beauty of those blossoming flowers remains in memory and seventy years on I still would thrill to see them again.

That was a visual memory but I can also recall memories of taste and smell. A couple of decades after rationing ended, a tin of lychees (litchis) came our way and as soon as I tasted the fruit and felt its texture I blurted out, 'Japan, we had these in Japan'. (They just might have been rambutans, a word from those days returning as I write.) After World War Two, in roaming the Highlands, there was the constant fight to keep the devil midges at bay. Remember Oil of Citronella? Remember flat round tins of *Dimp*? Nothing worked for long. Years on, in Tiso's shop in Rodney Street, Edinburgh, appeared what were called 'mosquito coils' which claimed to clear tents of the pests and many are the subsequent memories of gagging in the fug of the smoke released by the coils. They were marked 'Not to be used in enclosed spaces' but possible death by Moon Tiger seemed preferable to midge-induced insanity. I followed instructions the first time I used one of these, balancing the green coil on a small spiked metal stand and lighting the end, then blowing out the small flame to leave the resultant on-going smoke to get to work. My companion must have thought I'd gone bonkers that first time, for as soon as I smelt that smoke, I was babbling, 'Japan! Japan!' (Thinking about it now I rather suspect this would be in Malaya.)

Touch too has its memories. A cabinet shelf held a collection of tiny animal carvings in what I now know was jade. I was allowed to play with these, no doubt making up imaginative stories as kids do, but the memory is of the *feel* of the pieces, their smooth, cool, mysterious nature. I still stop to gaze in shop windows if I see jade *netsuke*.

Passing an antique shop in Edinburgh's Victoria Street in about 1970 I stopped in my tracks. There was something taking me straight back to Japan: a Mabel Lucie Attwell plaque which had hung in the bathroom, showing a twee figure and a rhyme:

'Please remember – don't forget/ Never leave the bathroom wet/ Nor leave the soap still in the water/ That's a thing we *never* ought'er ...'

I'm sure many of a certain vintage could complete the words. Of course I went in and bought it.

4

Maiden Voyage

We left Japan on February 4 1941, on what was 'Voyage Number One' (Maiden voyage) of the *SS President Monroe,* one of the US President Line ships – and a very luxurious liner at that. (The liner had been launched in Newport, Virginia on August 7, 1940). We called in to Shanghai, in China, February 6, Hong Kong, February 9, Manila in the Philippine Islands, February 11 and reached Singapore on February 19. Singapore was to fall on the following February 15. We had a year.

Mother scribbled letters over all the space available on a couple of the *President Monroe's* large, picturesque menu cards (described below) and these were kept. They give a glimpse of what life was like on an American liner. The first letter reports a stay with Chartered staff in Hong Kong. Port calls were a more leisurely affair in those days, today's business pressures unimaginable.

5 February 1941.
To Ian from Mother. Don't these boats in the picture [on the menu cover] look ridiculously unreal? Yet we have seen lots like them, only not so clean, that's the only difference, the real ones always look old and dirty. They are jolly good, seaworthy boats. The hills and temples in the background

are just like the real things in Japan, even if in reality they look grubby and old [the cover illustration of this book is based on one of these drawings].

We are having fine calm weather and are due in Shanghai tomorrow, where we hope to post this. Daddy got a bad cold and 103° temperature soon after leaving Kobe so has had a day in bed; aspirins and hot drinks made him sweat and feel much better tonight. Baby Davie is gorgeously well, sleeping better than ever, Hamish and I just couldn't be fitter. Hamish is getting very big and older looking and is having a grand time on this ship. There are several children about his size, so they have splendid play. He was very excited and came rushing to tell us 'Boy, oh boy, isn't it good there are so many children on this ship'. He is being very good although a bit too wild and gets so dirty. And he will say OK as often as possible – the American stewards are always saying it.

This is a beautiful new ship on its first voyage. The rooms are perfectly furnished and so comfy and the food is delicious and far too much of it. Our cabin is lovely, all four of us in it: two big beds and Hamish up in a bunk above Daddy's bed (double the size of old-fashioned bunks on board ships). Then lovely cupboards and dressing table and chairs and fitted carpet all over, everything the same colour, a nice fawn, bed-covers and even long curtains at port holes and very modern, attractive lights and mirror. Baby D sleeps in his own wee basket bed with his own pink and blue quilt. Our own bathroom is topping and fine for hanging up all the washing, and the babe's own bath stays there. Have a huge vase of roses someone gave us in Kobe.

The day we left we had Mr and Mrs Moffat and Mr Hare, the man we lived with there, to dinner on board, it was a nice change for them. Daddy ordered a ton of coal to be sent to him as a surprise present. We were four days there and it was terribly cold, tried to snow two of the days; four of us was a big extra in the house and everyone was so kind. So that's '*sayonara*' (good-bye) to Japan for us, wonder if we'll ever be back – hope so.

The next letter home was from Manila where there was more hospitality from the Chartered's eastern fraternity. They are still hoping Gran and Ian could come out, away from Scotland and German raids, but at this stage just don't know what would happen. Japan was obviously enjoyed ('Wonder if we'll ever be back – hope so') but also worrying – but not for what was really to happen. Britain went sleepwalking into the reality.

Manila 14 February.
To Gran, from Mother. Just posted a tiny letter to Ian today by clipper mail; it goes part of the way by air. All our letters will likely take ages to reach you. Four days here now, longer than expected and beginning to wish we were on the way again, the last lap. Interesting seeing this place, it's very spread out and a queer mixture; very American of course. We have spent two days with the McDougalls, he is in the Chartered here and we knew them in Colombo ages ago, then Mrs and the two girls of nine and eleven spent a day with us in Yokohama some months ago on their way through. They have a nice house and garden.

It seems terribly hot, a sudden change from cold weather in Hong Kong a few days ago. Billie and Hamish had their big coats on, on top of kilt and jersey (Ham) so suddenly this real tropical heat is a bit of a shock, only we don't care, as we're so thankful just to be all feeling really well again. Hamish had more fever and the ship's doctor gave him stuff that got rid of it quickly. But it pulled him down a lot. We all felt extra well in spite of excitement and being so busy and tired, then all getting wretched fevers and colds and Hamish losing his red cheeks so suddenly. All serene again. I'm my usual fit self although sleepy and hot. We'll soon become accustomed to the heat, the sudden change is what is so trying. We will have time to enjoy the sea once we sail, with a lovely swimming pool and three or four days to Singapore. David has been fit all the time and now wears hardly any clothes and doesn't seem to mind the heat. B is a big help getting bath ready and putting it away and carrying things, bathing Hamish etc. Managing nicely, but the stewards do so little on this line, they are mostly 'off duty,' especially in port. We were warned about the appalling service on American ships and am now sampling it but surviving quite cheerfully. Thinking all the time about you and wondering what house you are in. Sure you are delighted to have us out of Japan, nice as the country is, but the news is queer and everyone wonders these days, what will happen next. Feel lucky to be travelling as we are (not separating) but won't be happy until we are ALL together. Kept quite busy – thanking letters and yours are all I can manage.

The charming menu cards point to a different era. There's something so secure and certain in these cards, various staff named, the confident 'Voyage No 1. En Route to Manila', then to America. The menu listed twelve courses with nibbles of celery and green and black olives to start, and California Dates, after Dinner Mints, Fruit, and a Demi Tasse. I wonder how many more voyages there were before Pearl Harbour.

Several President Line ships appear in *Lloyds War Losses* but the *USS President Monroe* went on to have a distinguished war, ranging the Pacific, carrying troops, goods, fighter planes through the years and earning five 'battle

51

stars'. Having been converted to a cargo ship, and armed, by the end of the war she was in a sorry state. She took part in the Operation Magic Carpet in 1945, returning home the thousands of US troops in the East. In 1946 she was returned to the President Line. In 1965 she was sold to a Greek shipping line, becoming the SS *Marianna V* and eventually (always so sad) scrapped in 1973.

Klang 1941. The flat's roof garden. Hamish with David and Amah.

5

Klang, In Sunshine

Singapore (from the Sanskrit *lion-town*) had been acquired by the East India Company from the Sultan of Johor in 1819 and soon prospered as a key staging post in Britain's far eastern trade. Coming under the Colonial Office in 1867 Singapore continued to grow and dominate trade as the exploitation of tin developed the long length of Malaya with its few 'Straits Settlements'. At that time Klang was a local fort and Kuala Lumpur a grass-roofed Chinese village. The leap from then to 1940 is only matched by the history of 1940 to the present. Frank Swettenham[3] was the first to penetrate river, swamps and jungle to reach Kuala Lumpur – in search of a girl who had been trafficked between Chinese secret societies. He failed in that mission but had his first taste of a world that suited his bold yet skilled ways. Kuala Lumpur would become a boom town from the tin mining (rubber came later) and the Selangor Residency, originally in Klang, moved to Kuala Lumpur. Frank Swettenham became Resident in 1882. In 1896, as Resident General, he would create Kuala Lumpur as the Straits capital. (The population today is well over a million.) Self-satisfied Singapore regarded living 'up country' as being in the sticks but my parents preferred it. Not that mother couldn't enjoy the social life when available.

As will be seen in the letters following, there was a busy social life despite (or because of) the growing concerns about the political situation. I recall almost nothing of this. Before finding the letters my awareness of what went on came from my mother's 1941 pocket diary (to which she added notes at the back into the following May and the conclusion of our family saga.) Most of the entries are simply recording names of friends and arranging dates for *tiffin*, tennis, riding, club and, more than anything else, Mah Jongg[4]. In the first week in 'sweltering Singapore' father had one doctor visit and no doubt briefings at the Chartered Bank HQ. They spent the week in the Adelphi Hotel, with much finding and dining with old friends and, for mother, essential shopping and being shown round (Botanic Gardens, Reservoir, etc), enjoying the Club and swimming – and 'the pictures'.

For the next year the cinema was almost a weekly ritual (there was very little other cultural or intellectual stimulus). They never went to the cinema once back home in Scotland. A few noted in the diary: *Night Train to Munich, Shop Around the Corner, Mr Smith goes to Washington, Daytime Wife, Spring Parade, Wuthering Heights, Strike Up the Band, Footsteps in the Dark, the Great Dictator, All This and Heaven Too, The Four Feathers* and a Shirley Temple. Sweetie Shirley Temple set my boy's teeth on edge and *The Four Feathers* thrilled – my very first cinematic memory the seeming thousands of horsemen charging into battle in the noise and dust of the desert. Performances of course always ended with everyone standing for 'God Save the King'.

At some time, somewhere, I took part in a production of *Peter Pan* – with hindsight an apt choice with Japan about to destroy this Neverland. The idea of being overtaken by complete disaster never registered. All I can remember about

Peter Pan was sitting on a mattress, on stage, in pyjamas, as one of twins and disgracing myself, off-stage, by pulling off Hook's hook just before he made an entrance. Could this really have been in the Christmas holidays, from which there would have been no return to school? But some more on the political and military situation is called for before reading the innocent letters from and to Malaya.

Britain between the World Wars was in no position to construct enough warships to have both a European fleet, and one in the Far East to counter the rising power of Japan. Seeing no remedy it was easiest to close eyes to the problem. 'A battle fleet would be sent when required' was mere myth in face of the resurgence of German naval power and admitted as such on the outbreak of World War Two. So how could Singapore be defended? The fallacious belief that jungle would defend the landward side saw great guns positioned to face any seaborne attack. Lord Trenchard on the other hand argued for a strong RAF presence with torpedo bombers, fighters and reconnaissance aircraft. The planners however did not believe that planes could sink warships. Some airfields were constructed up the length of Malaya. The assumption remained however that Britain intrinsically believed its naval power far exceeded that of Japan. In 1939 Britain had 15 (often outdated) capital ships and Japan had 10 (modernised or new) and, more importantly, as the Japanese realised, they had six aircraft carriers (and 11 being built) against Britain's 7 (and 4 being built) – none of which went east till much later in the War. The German war took priority. By 1940 London recognised the air defence of Singapore as being vital, but did nothing until the end of 1941, when troops rather than planes were sent. Aid which might have been sent was diverted by Churchill in June 1941 to the Soviet Union following the German invasion. Instead of a promised 336 planes (against a demanded 566) when Japan struck there were only 158 low quality aircraft in place. When the Japs invaded they had 300 tanks, we had none. The sending of the *Prince of Wales* and *Repulse* as an unprotected deterrent was another Churchill blunder. The *Prince of Wales* was modern but under-gunned (14" while America preferred 16" and the Japanese 18"), *Repulse* a modernised WW1-designed battlecruiser. The aircraft carrier *Indomitable* which was to accompany them ran aground in the West Indies. The two warships reached Singapore on December 4, a tremendous morale booster and symbol of Britain's powers. When they were sunk on December 10 it gave a contrary, devastating blow to morale. Britain's preconceptions about Japan proved terribly wrong in every way. (Churchill admitted, 'The violence, fury, skill and input of Japan far exceeded anything we had been led to expect' – though, when visiting President Roosevelt in August 1941, he had boasted 'if they do [invade] they will find they have bitten off more than they can chew'.) The Japanese invaded through the north of Malaya on December 7 and Singapore fell on February 15, seeing the largest single loss of troops in British imperial history. One account I've read likened it to our loss of the American colonies following Cornwallis's surrender at Yorktown in 1781.

An early traveller described Malaya's climate of heat and humidity (90° by day, 80° at night) as 'impossible for ladies' quite apart from the 'presence of snakes, mosquitoes, beetles, earwigs, and ants (some an inch long).' The climate would not be any better in 1941 (or 2017) but the nasties have steadily declined as urbanisation, industrialisation and rural cultivation usurps their territory. October to December is the rainy season and, of course, it was assumed there could be no Japanese attack launched at that season (wrong again). The climate was 'difficult,' 'a daily sweatbath,' 'sapping energy and intellect' so the comfortable nature of traditional social life was a needed escape. A *stengah* (whisky and soda) was earned, the Club ritual a counter to depression.

I'm surprised there are still rumblings about Gran and Ian joining the family. I've a cable (telegram) sent to Gran in Carrick (received 5.3.41): 'Now stationed Klang. Unlikely you Ian permitted to come here. Writing. Browns'. On the 6.3.42 mother would receive a telegram from father in Colombo: 'Lost everything but safe love Brown'. The year between is what follows.

The letters have had some pruning, of much that is peripheral, the many repetitions, the family endearments and so on. I have also added the occasional full stop or introduced a new paragraph. Mother wrote as she spoke, in a cheery *continuo*.

We lived in a flat on top of the Chartered's building, which dominated the town's wide, palm-edged streets. I've no memory of it. Just another place where the family lived. No doubt it was comfortable and there would be servants. The Club was nearby and the capital, Kuala Lumpur (K.L.) only an hour's drive away. We had reached Klang on the first of March but only one letter (following) survives from early days. Settling in would not present any problems. I was sent 'up-country' to school, and it was finally realised Ian and Gran could not travel out to join us.

Klang. 15 April 1941.
To Ian, from Father. Had a nice letter from you yesterday sent on by Singapore. We should soon be getting them direct to Klang. Hamish was a clever lad on the last day of the tennis tournament. It came on very heavy rain just at the end and many people were caught in the shelter by the

The view from the bank in Klang, 1941.

courts unable to return to the Club till Hamish came to the
rescue with umbrellas. He went back and forwards with
them for about half an hour and got all the people over dry.
He got soaked but it did not matter as he only wore a cotton
romper and went straight home afterwards.

[Mother added:] The money raised went to war funds.
Our visitors won three prizes, splendid players. Hamish got
a big Easter egg on Sunday but was more thrilled by having
people in the house. He slept on a couch to let others have

his room. They all thought David wonderful: never cried and smiled all the time.

This was written on the cover of the programme of the Klang Club's Easter 1941 annual tournament, held in aid of 'FMS [Federated Malay States] War Fund'. (Churchill glowers through the strings of a tennis racquet and Hitler and Mussolini mark a map of Europe). No letters survive for the next few months.

Klang, 23 July 1941.
To Gran, from Mummy. Had a lovely weekend up in the Cameron Highlands with Hamish. Found the lad very fit and delighted with everything. We collected him on Saturday morning and he was allowed to stay all the time with us seeing we were in a house (if we'd been in hotel he'd have had to go back to school each night). We all thoroughly enjoyed it. He looks much better although too thin still for my liking but so full of energy and so talkative and noisy as ever. He really does like school and the Mother Superior is a dear, not too solemn and the weans are splendidly looked after, the place is beautiful with stylish buildings and grounds.

The house was new, with a lovely garden not quite finished, also hens and near a lovely big burn. Arrived on Friday night after quite an exciting bit of journey up the winding steep last 30 miles in pouring rain. 180 miles from K.L. Some bits so winding that it makes hard going. Delighted with the car and *syce* [driver]. But what rain!

Very hilly, nice country, not opened up much. Like Ceylon and India, mostly jungle on the big hills, once the lower country where rubber grows is left, so a complete change to other places we've seen. No flat bits high up, just masses of high hills. Walked a lot and played about in garden and paddling in different rivers, went a long drive to have tea with friends one afternoon, but the winding roads makes most people feel ill, especially children. What a splendid appetite Hamish has. Took him lots of chocolates and his new socks and he certainly enjoyed seeing us. Even socks have to have Cash's name tabs sewn on them, never mind the six shirts, six shorts, etc. Delighted to have had the few days in the cool, having a fire at night and blankets on beds – very cold nights and early mornings and then really hot in the sun in day time. Little house with everything supplied and a splendid cook; paid so much a day and then will have a bill for rent; cheaper than hotel and suited us much better. Time simply flies. David isn't getting his 10 o'clock feed tonight for the first time so hope he doesn't object!

Klang 29 July, to Gran from Mummy. Expect you will have got our cable by now (about school) longing to get your one after you fix up. Thinking about you two always but now more so than ever because of the school problem; once again different plans must be made.

I know how relieved you will be that we aren't in Japan now if real war comes of the Indo-China move, as we fear it is bound to. It's a nasty experience for the 'foreigners' left there, very few British and Americans compared to the number of Japs in Canada and America, far less with others in Britain. They'd surely be swopped and if not, far more Japs to suffer than the other side, only we would treat and feed them far too well compared to what they would do to our people, as they simply haven't got the stuff and their country is in a rotten state, so hope it's never a case of internment. Feel angrier with the Vichy French [who allowed Japanese troops to be stationed in their colonies] than these fools of Japs, what they have let themselves in for when the country isn't in a state to finish China off without tackling so much more. They will certainly help Germany. Poor blighters in France maybe couldn't do anything else but surely the colonies could have held out and become Free French; that part seems disgraceful. Indo-China could easily have got help from us if they'd held out. You get enough war on wireless and newspapers so better not write much about it!

2 August.
To Gran, from Mummy. What a fine quick letter we have just got and the lovely snaps. Glad you had some warm weather and outings in the boat. You all look splendid in the snaps; how big the two weans are, Ian more so than Margaret. They make a nice-looking pair.

Last night to a cocktail party on board 'something' in Port Swettenham five miles from here. Nice to be on a British ship again, especially a useful one and they were all so jolly and kind and make splendid hosts, just drinks and wee eats and their splendid band playing and a little dancing. Of course we danced. They are so delighted to see any women again. There are too many of the same in Singapore for the civilians to bother much about them, so they enjoy putting in at small places, but never can tell how long for, so things have just to be arranged hurriedly, just games and wee parties. Came home at ten after enjoying the stunt, arranged to play tennis with two of them today and bring them home for dinner. It's wonderful how something is always cropping up to keep us very pleasantly busy. The time flies. David is simply so proud of being able to sit up quite steadily and not topple over. He weighs 19 lbs.

4 August
Another weekend over and quite a busy one. We played tennis on Saturday with our Navy men and instead of two,

61

we had six officers to dinner here, after a little sing-song at Club. They did appreciate everything. Then yesterday Reids' (lunch on to afternoon tea), then tennis, badminton, clock-golf. They had four Australian soldiers and a lot of important Malays and a Scots couple, an interesting mixture.

There were we three British women in tennis clothes, all legs and five or six Malay ladies all dressed up, so very well covered. They are prettier than Siamese but not nearly so westernised, hardly ever speak English (one of them did and that was most unusual), none of them play strenuous games and they are kept in the background much more than the Siamese. They aren't shocked at our ways, just realise we have different ideas and love meeting up. Two of them come to the weekly knitting parties and they are all very pleasant and chatter away and smile and laugh with us. Two men yesterday were very like the Siamese princes we knew, with perfect English and they played tennis. Very pleasant. Then there were grandparents with a wee granddaughter, absolutely spoilt and dreadful English clothes on the baby, still using a bottle and a dreadful dummy. Grandfather was the heir to the Sultan of Perak (another state; here is Selangor). We are going to play tennis and have Australian soldiers for dinner one day soon. So few Europeans bother about them except in the big towns like K.L. and they seem very decent.

5 August

Told you after our visit to Cameron Highlands that it was a consolation to see no very big boys at school there, plenty very big girls but no boys. Some who came out here from home last year before the new restrictions were sent or taken to Australia to school as there's nothing suitable here, so that's a consolation to us, that Ian didn't come out. Think Nuwara Eliya big school is much better (in Ceylon) than either of the two here. Perfectly all right for Ham's age of course.

Aren't we learning to have a lot of patience these days? The people who lose all their possessions in [German] raids makes you think it's a good thing not to have many these days. Isn't that a consolation? Think about 'Caledonia' and parting with all your precious stuff and yet, on the whole, I do think you are better to be free of it all, free of that much worry and able to move suddenly. No ties. Wonder if you got more evacuees, or if Carrick is too unhandy?

By Jove, how mending piles up when one hasn't a sewing machine. I'm getting letters off before Ham's holidays and would like to borrow a machine to feel free to have lots of time with him.

I have just come in from a wonderful ride, a real treat. Mrs Speedin is young and awfully nice and had a huge lovely breakfast for us after being on the horses for two hours with lots of gallops and quick cantering. Mrs Bree came from Port Swettenham and took me the half hour out to Speedins'. We both just loved the ride.

We listen umpteen times a day to the news, which is rather queer these days but must just wait and see.

5 August
To Ian, from Mummy. We were delighted to get the snaps in the quickest mail ever, well under two months on the way is a record. You all look splendid in the snaps and how big Margaret and you have got since we left home.

You asked about the Sultan's Palace on the stamps. It is very near here and is very much occupied and has armed guards at the lodge at the beginning of the private road into the grounds. We met and played with one of the Sultan's sons on Sunday at a tennis tea-party in Mr and Mrs Reid's. He invited us to play tennis yesterday at the *astana* (that's what the Palace is called) but it rained, so that was a wash-out. Our flat above the Bank is very big and nice but it's too hot and noisy. It is one of the biggest buildings in the place and is at the very edge of the town, so is the cinema, then there is the golf course and Club and this fancy Palace at the other side of the golf course, so on one side we are nice and country-ish and all town on the other side.

We were at a topping party on a ship one night, then we played tennis with some of the officers and six of them came home to dinner with us. Hamish often does very quick drawings like these [in the letter], entirely on his own. He wouldn't take advice even if anyone gave him any, but he really has good ideas. He often does much better battle scenes than this, but I thought you would like to see his ideas. Usually the Nazi Cross is much plainer on the sinking ships or aeroplanes on fire; they are always getting the worst of the fight naturally! This morning he has been cutting out triangular bandages with me. I have twenty yards of material to make forty bandages, a yard square, cut across for each one, then they have to be hemmed.

9 August. To Gran, from Mummy. Hamish has been in the isolation ward for a week or so, with ringworm spots, so do hope he is better by his birthday and able to eat his cake in company. He is very well with it and out all the time, has a special wee bit of garden for his very own and is taken walks. Of course they have to be very careful of infection and we know he gets the best of attention.

The big cinemas are air-conditioned but give rather too drastic a change from the usual sticky heat, so if it's nice to feel cool and dry for a wee while it's dashed dangerous for catching chills, going in all sweaty and suddenly feeling nearly frozen. There aren't many degrees difference in actual temperature: it's the dryness which is such a sudden change. Davie is certainly not spoilt, has his regular hours for everything and only gets his playing at the right times. He is hours alone in play pen, perfectly happy.

11 August
Have just been to the station to buy comics to put in Ham's parcel, posting today. Came back to find mail from you and now I'm trying to write on my knees with Peter, the big kitten playing all over me and always making a dive for the pen. Did you give anyone roots of your Macedonia before leaving 'Caledonia'?

14 August
I'm knitting away at the fine grey cable-stitch sweater for Ian, also one for a sailor and have a pile of mending waiting.

News is queer; surprised at nothing these days and certainly can't look far ahead. The Russians are doing well and at last we are getting some of our own back, in raiding Germany. No use wondering how things are going to go out east – will see soon enough. Seems maybe lucky that we couldn't get permits for you to come out, much as we hate the separation. It's nothing compared to what lots of folks have to put up with.

Ham's birthday yesterday, so wonder how he got on. He'd like his parcel and I'm posting a colouring book to him today as he loves pictures to colour, useful if he is still in isolation. Maybe they would keep the cake etc until his spots are better, as they give nice little parties on birthdays.

I am simply furious at myself at my knitting, have just this minute ripped out all the back of Ian's grey sweater. Waited until it was right up to a shoulder before discovering back was too narrow, so out it came. Played golf yesterday, after being out to Mah Jongg tea in morning at McGanns, on their Bukit Rajah Estate. Billie has played strenuous tennis three afternoons running so we are getting lots of exercise these days.

The Australians loved their dinner with us on Monday, sent them home in car at twelve o'clock, after they'd seen a lovely plant that only flowers for a few hours on one night. Each flower looks like a gorgeous white water lily but grows out of dry-looking leaves. Had sixteen flowers all on the one plant. Moon flower, or *keng-wah* it's called and is simply lovely, although only flowering for half a night once a month. The buds appear same time as new moon and usually open after the moon is full. We are quite proud to have improved this one so much and it was lucky having a party the very night it flowered. They all raved about it and loved having a civilised meal for a change. One is a young Australian padre who joined up as a private and is now a sergeant, another had a good job in his father's big merchant's business and used to buy silk from Japan. They enjoyed the tennis. Davie was at Club that afternoon and got lots of attention, but he is just as well in his pen on the roof where he usually is in afternoons.

23 August

Have just received your cable this morning, after deciding that it couldn't be going to come until next month. Relieved that you are staying put. Hope another year will find us all together and everything much more settled, whether or not the war [in Europe] gets finished, but daren't count on leave or anything these days. You are in as good a place as you could possibly be for quiet nights and good food, and good friends and sharing rations must make your coupons go further. Dollar is maybe too full these days and Carrick school maybe not big enough and yet impossible to find the perfect place these days.

Hamish is due home tomorrow – meeting him at train in

K.L. at six tomorrow evening. We had a nice time at Philps' last night for tea, after B went to dentist and I shopped. Oh their kids are desperately disobedient, only 4½ and 2½ but couldn't be more spoilt, the mother's fault entirely, nice clever weans simply ruined. How strict we feel in comparison; worth it too. Please don't spoil Ian, although he seems to be awfully good. You are quite proud of him eh! David stood alone hanging on to play-pen bars the other day, he is terribly strong and bright, still sleeps a lot and has completely given up bottle, isn't that clever at only eight months? He gets Cow & Gate every meal of course, porridge or soup before his drink of milk and he now loves his rusks too. Hardly any hair yet which is just as well, as it's so hot. It's a job trying to keep him clear of prickly heat; he is so active and gets very hot. We use special soap and plenty special powder, also TCP. Hope Ham's ringworm is better; frighted in case he hands it on to the baby. It's not nearly such a bad thing to get out here as at home, it's milder and very common but seems hard to get rid of all the same. It's well worth having been separated from Hamish for a while to see the big improvement on his appearance – good colour again.

28 August 1941.
To Ian, from Father. We have got Hamish back with us now and he is looking very well. All the Kuala Lumpur children came down in two carriages on the train and it looked such a crowd when they all got out. They had to go over forty miles in a bus from Cameron Highlands down to Tapah where the railway is and then about five hours in the train to K.L.'s big station. Some of the children had been sick in the bus and Hamish said they spilt it all over the seat. It's a very winding road down 6000 feet of hill and Hamish was very pleased that he had not been sick.

He has holidays for a month just now and then a longer holiday at Christmas, when the weather even down here is cooler.

K.L.'s station was built in grand imperial style, as were most governmental buildings, so K.L. was an impressive sight. (Even in Klang the Palace, Club and Bank dominated.) Could people possibly have envisaged the K.L. of today with its 1483 feet high Petronas Towers and the other skyscrapers of a metropolis? In 2016 K.L. was the seventh most visited city in the world by tourists (12.02 million) – and Singapore was sixth (12.11 million).

Cameron Highlands. 28 August.
To Gran and Ian from Hamish. I hope you both are very well. I would like to have you both here in Klang. We are very well and I am on holiday from Cameron Highlands. I have a Meccano set and it is a small set and has many coloured pieces, green, red, gold, silver, and one is rusty and I am sad. The funniest is the wheel and nuts.

Klang. 18 September.
To Ian, from Mummy. You have asked several times how big a place Kuala Lumpur is; well it's small compared to Singapore, which is a huge, busy place now, even compared to a few years ago. K.L. is a good bit smaller than Colombo even but enormous compared to Klang.

The fruit here is like what we used to get in Bangkok and Colombo: plenty bananas, guavas, pineapples, papayas all the time and chikos, mangos, mangosteens, durian, pomelos, tree tomatoes and some others at certain seasons. (Think I have forgotten some) Apples and oranges have to be cold stored. So plenty fruit here; wish you could get as much. Many more different kinds in Japan where we had all the home fruits, plus all the tropical ones, as well as some others like figs and melons. It never seemed too cold for us in Japan as the winter was so dry and sunny. Here it feels damp all the time, much more so than Colombo. We are all very fit and always seem to be busy. David is trying hard to walk. Hamish will soon be going back to school. He doesn't like the idea of that too well but doesn't make a fuss about it. It will be good for him to get back to the cool. Daddy has some fine stamps for you this mail. How big your collection is growing! Daddy's collection is in Colombo with most of our other belongings. He still collects new British Colonies. We now have 150ft of film taken in this country and the same amount taken in Japan, with borrowed cameras so that will help to keep the record of the Brown boys on 'wall pictures what moves' as Hamish called the ciné film.

Wrote a bit of your mail days ago because I knew we'd be busy during the blackout and air raid practises. I was helping at a canteen from midnight until 6am one night, quite near here, so we walked there in the dark. Daddy came along with us. Two Chinese girls were helping along with me and we were kept busy making cocoa and tea, and marmite, etc plus bread, butter and jam and giving it to wardens and all the workers. Next night I had an early, easier spell, Daddy and all the house servants took turn about all night in watching for 'fires'. Tonight is the last night of this blackout.

We are going to see a Shirley Temple film this afternoon, then a tea-party here, with the Oliver family, then Capt Sheppard is bringing his projector and we'll all see our own efforts. Oliver is bringing us a new kitten; hope Peter will not be jealous. Hamish is going to Port Swettenham to play with some children tomorrow, Saturday, out to the rubber estate, where the horse is, and then off to school on Sunday, so a busy few days to finish up with. He got a sting on his toe yesterday from a hornet. It was very sore and his whole foot is still swollen. The stamps in his letter are from him. He says we mustn't mix them with the ones Daddy sends. Hamish likes to give David his orange or some food and he is very proud of his wee brother, also his big one, he is always talking about you, Ian pet.

18 September.
To Ian, from Daddy. Hamish goes back to school on Sunday and we will motor up to Kuala Lumpur to put him on the train. All the children go up together on the same train and one of the teachers looks after them. The school is about 6000 feet up so it is nice and cool. Hamish got stung on the toe by a hornet. Poor kid his foot is still very swollen but it will soon get better. We had a day at the sea on Sunday at Morib about 28 miles away but it was very wet and we had to have our picnic in the car. It was quite nice bathing in the sea in the rain but not very nice afterwards. Hope you are having a good time in Carrick. Mummy posted a Xmas parcel for you, and Margaret's will go tomorrow. Have you been able to get a bike yet?

Klang 25 September 1941.
To Ian, from Mummy. Hamish never finished this drawing but he was so keen on 'camouflaged cars'. He had seen a lot lately and he thought the colours were just the stuff. He always hoo-rahed and saluted when soldiers drove past and loved when they saluted back. He seems to be nicely settled at school again, and should be getting his pink cheeks back. You will know the Clyde jolly well, going to so many places and you seem to have had lovely times seeing all the relations and friends again, as well as new people and new places. Thanks ever so much for all your nice long letters. Hope Gran and you feel nicely settled and have no more

70

puzzlings about schools. We do hope the old Dalton plan lessons are a great success. [The Dalton Plan was a secondary education system based on individual learning.]

I had a grand ride yesterday with Mrs Bree and Mrs Speedin on the latter's horses. David William Bree is two years old; hasn't he almost the same name as our David William Brown?

The new kitten Hamish christened Shirley Jane is now perfectly settled and happy. Our Peter didn't like her for the first two days, jealous I suppose, now he plays beautifully with her all the time. Hamish christened them both with water on their foreheads, in the bathroom, talking away all the time. We weren't at the ceremony but heard him.

P.S. Purple thing in this drawing [of Hamish's] is evidently a shell and the awful red thing a hand grenade exploding. I thought it was the sun, but it is setting (as per Hamish's usual) behind a hill, maybe Fuji.

1 October.
To Ian, from Mummy. I'm trying to write on our bit of flat roof, but can't get on with it for gazing at David in his playpen, so contented and active. He has three teeth now and three more are almost through; they seem to be a bit sore but he is never off his food or sleep and perfectly happy. He is trying to walk and makes lovely wee noises – talking.

2 October.
To Ian, from Daddy. Here are some more stamps for you and some very nice ones too. I don't think you have the Rs.5 Indian one. We were glad to hear all about your holiday in Largs and your visit to Millport. I just wish we could all have been there. Mummie has been out riding this morning again and has just come back. I am going to the Baha Hae Factory this afternoon to see them making shoes. They

make thousands every day and send them all over this part of the world. They have a very big up to date place here and are always very busy. Czechs run it and they are a very nice crowd.

6 October 1941.
To Gran, from Mummy. A Mrs Paton came in unexpectedly to give us news of Hamish. She and her husband had been in Camerons for about three weeks holiday, seeing their boy in same school and same age as Hamish and they fell in love with our lad, said he was always so bright and friendly. Still the gate-crashing wee bully; but they said not at all cheeky with all his talk, inviting them all to come to the Chartered Bank, Klang, during next holiday and so proud of both brothers and telling them everything imaginable and so amusing. They have two sons and a daughter at Dollar, day pupils, wonder if Ian knows the name? Eldest is boy of maybe fourteen, then they have a girl here, same age as David, so am sure we'll be visiting backwards and forwards; they live over twenty miles away, quite near the place Morib where we bathe. They have a house in Dollar and I think an aunt looking after them. Seems a very nice family. Rubber planting[5] out here and five is a pretty hefty family these days. Odd meeting someone else with a Dollar connection.

We had dinner one night with Capt Sheppard, pilot in port Swettenham, and saw his ciné films, Budge [a longtime friend, Budge Stiven] enjoyed seeing our ones too, then another night he came and had a meal here, terrific talker and very amusing. Have been getting new sheeting for David, also green mosquito netting for a big new net for him. Our rooftop home is less bothered by *poochies* [insects/creepy-crawlies] than bungalows out in the estate. Have aertex to make him pyjamas and rompers so should be quite busy soon.

Budge is finding it very hard to know what to do, it's dreadful for her these complicated war days. If she leaves this country, she couldn't get in again but she wants to see the parents. So much has happened to Budge since she came. Yesterday we had a busy day, she dearly loves shopping, we got green sheets and pillow slips, cheap cotton things but very attractive for her room here. Our guest room looks nicer with only the one bed in it. Always odd things to get for the flat and that is Bank pigeon, we have plenty of our own odds and ends. Nursery designs on cotton, blue ground for wee rompers for David and B was hunting for stuff to have dungarees made for a friend's child. It takes such a lot of time hunting in all the shops for something that just can't be got. This time it was leather pram braces for David; will have to get them made. Had a delicious *tiffin* at Howard's and a scrounge round the nice garden. Before that we met him in K.L. and went to his rubber estate, only five miles away but seems right in the wilds, saw some old Bangkok photos and had a very good meal and chat. Did some K.L. shopping, my slacks to tailor to be tightened, hunting for the pram braces for David and comics for Hamish, then back here after five, had tea, then we went a walk and into Club, so it felt quite a full day. David's new teeth coming are worrying him a lot, not that it affects his sleeping or eating but can see by the things he does with his mouth and unusual wee screeches he gives.

Are you being anxious to get Ian back to Dollar? Do they need to go on waiting list for day pupils? If so, perhaps it would be wise to put him on list as day boy and could you get digs on a farm or anywhere near? You said every corner was full up when you tried before. Good luck to '42.

In a wee note to Ian at this time – October – mother ended, 'Heaps of love and good luck in 1942, as it will be next year by the time this arrives'. In 1941 what was to come obviously held no over-great worry and where they'd be in 1942 unimaginable.

Some of my weekly letters from the Cameron Highlands were kept, along with slips from the school giving weekly reports. A typical letter from me: 'It rains every evening so we go for handwork after tea ... We are now learning some Christmas songs. I shall sing them to you when I go home ... Last Saturday was so sunny that we all went for a little picnic instead of classes ... We are very excited because next weekend is the Exhibition and Sale. Could you please send me some money for the Sale ...' Every letter has patriotic war drawings in garish colours, with just the odd one showing flowers.

24 October.

To Ian, from Mummy. We are having a very busy time just now, having Budge Stiven with us, she would be Auntie Margaret to Hamish and you, as Budge was her young pet name, wonder if you remember her, her parents are Browns. She thinks David is the best baby she has ever seen and he certainly is 'all that could be adsired' as Hamish used to say for desired, but then you and Hamish were both terribly good infants as well but think you all become noisy and wild after a year and a half old. That's our family likeness!

We have been watching some rugger, this is the season for it here. Long to hear how you are getting on at school, if you are quite happy with the queer way of doing lessons. I'm finishing off a pair of stockings for you now and they are too big for me, so think they should fit you all right, allowing a little for shrinking. We had a nice bathe and picnic yesterday at Morib, very quiet one without the Ham – our first for ages. It is very hot here but we are happy – although hating being separated from you and Gran but that is the war's fault, not ours.

24 October.
To Ian, from Daddy. Yesterday we went down to the sea at Morib and had a nice day bathing. We were all day there and are very sunburned today. That beach is 28 miles away to the south and is the only possible bathing place near here. It is not very good as the water is very shallow and the tide goes miles out so it is practically impossible to get out of your depth and there are no rocks to dive from. Not like Colombo's lovely clear open sea, but it is the best we can get. Port Swettenham is only 4½ miles away but it is all mud, swamp and crocodiles so is no use for bathing. Hamish seems to be getting on nicely. His last reports said that he works very well but talks too much. Isn't that funny? There are a few more stamps for you but nothing special this time.

By now Hideki Tojo had become Japanese Prime Minister – while keeping on as War Minister – to become the driving force behind the move for a series of pre-emptive hits against colonial powers, including the American Pacific fleet. In early November secret orders were in place for the attack on Pearl Harbour. Diplomatic visits to Washington were as much a smoke screen as anything else. Japan had to have access to a wide range of resources, but particularly oil.

30 October.
To Ian, from Mummy. We have had a letter from Daddy's sister Nellie, who was in Cyprus and she and her husband are now in Durban, where Jim and family are; Jim is her brother and Daddy's brother as well of course. Jim is a

soldier now and was one in the last war too. [Little did mother know she would be joining all these relations in Durban in a few months' time.]

Here we are all well, David has got one more tooth through and has 4 more bothering him but is as cheery and smilie as ever. Hamish is well and his reports have been very good. You have a jolly good, big, stamp collection, and the extra ones will be useful for swapping some day when you meet other people interested.

We enjoyed hearing from a friend in Canada who used to be in Yokohama and is in Montreal now. Our relations and friends get moved about a lot, don't they?

Rosemount, Carrick Castle 1 November 1941.
To Mummy and Daddy, from Ian. This week Gran and I have had eight lovely letters from you. They arrived all the days of the week. I will answer four just now for I do not know where Gran has the others. Hamish writes very good letters. How do you like the car? Are you rationed for petrol? [They were. Rice too was rationed.] I do not exchange stamps here except with Margaret sometimes and I have given her a lot of stamps as well. Nobody else collects stamps. There are only 8 boys and 6 girls in the school. The 100 fish we caught in the day were mackerel. We took them to everybody in the village. [Ian and I would do this in autumn 1944, once reunited.] The post has brought two more letters from you. Thank you very much for all the stamps. Ten letters in one week is a lot. This morning Margaret and I were helping Aunt Dorothy in the garden. Can David walk? I was very slow to get my teeth when I was a baby. The silver mug I had has been very useful.

With love and best of luck, from your biggest son.

Carrick. 9 November.
To Mummy and Daddy, from Ian. I hope David has a very nice [December 15] birthday. Gran and I have sent David's birthday card and your Christmas cards a good time ago and hope they arrive in time. Yesterday was Poppy Day. There was snow on the hills a day or two ago, yesterday was very frosty and today is windy and raining. Hutton's auxiliary cruiser which was called *Minnie Haha* broke loose and sank. Davie Ballantyne found the boom and the boat hook on the shore. I am getting on at school alright. Miss Livingstone said my writing was improving. What is Hamish's favourite subject? Mine is Arithmetic and I like Geography a bit. At school we go in at ten o'clock and come out at four o'clock. Last night Aunt Dorothy was baking and can bake very well.

Chartered Bank, Klang. 10 November 1941.
To Gran from Mummy. We were out last night to the *astana*, the palace (near the Mosque that is on the Selangor stamps) for part of the wedding ceremonies of a young couple; she is a daughter of the late Sultan, heaven knows how many of them he had but he had 48 sons officially! It was quite interesting and colourful and the clothes so totally different from any others. We all got rice and also eggs in attractive little baskets (paper but beautifully made). All unusual to us so very interesting. The building is very nice inside, good red carpets and plenty ceiling fans and a queer special thing for the couple to sit in, all lit up with coloured lights, ditto the lovely big double stairway.

Imposing building, stands on a hill and the golf course and Club are alongside. Some tiny paths cross the golf course and we often have to be careful not to hit people walking or on bikes! That snap [p58], taken from our verandah is across the square and only to big shops. The dirt and smells are awful sometimes but the architecture looks grand in a picture! The railway station and big hotel in K.L. are the same type, very imposing and picturesque; dreadful waste really. We've had a lot of rain lately, so few games. Went a walk after tea yesterday. Today there is a stint in Club for Poppy Fund and we have all been collecting: an easy beat for me, only our own bank. Missed riding last week, as it was the day Budge left and I went with her to K.L.

I've just finished the most awkward parcel I've ever made and the brute has been returned from post office two miserable ounces over the allowed 5lbs. No one downstairs in the office could pack it, such dreadful shapes, mostly because of the stocking stretchers. We thought they would be useful these days of rationing to help keep precious hand-knitted wool stockings from shrinking after washing. You put stockings on stretchers and leave until dry. Hope the bally things arrive whole. Dark grey stockings with red tops should be quite nice with Ian's pullover. There was also chocolate biscuits and butter, etc. If we are ever evacuated, of course we will cable you at once – don't think it will come to that though.

13 November

I've just been to the station bookstall to get comics for Hamish; scarce and hard to get now. That wee walk has made me so hot I will rush and bath in a minute and be ready for Doctor Swift coming in to see our cat. We had drinks with him in his garden last night after we'd been for a walk. I was saying we'd have to get a vet but he offered to have a look first. Riding tomorrow, collecting wool from Mrs Reid's on Sat morning and having a mob for *tiffin* on Sunday after Church, plus rugger match on Sat and I think Budge and Howard to dinner, so I don't see any mending or David's rompers or new mosquito net being made in the next week!

It seems ridiculous how the time passes so quickly and yet we do nothing important. Raining nearly every afternoon so there's very little tennis or golf. We sometimes manage a walk. David now often walks two or three steps before collapsing. We don't encourage him – just eleven months old. I was out to Gray's estate playing Mah Jongg yesterday morning and took back her sewing machine at last, as Mrs Reid has left me hers to use while they are on leave. They go off next week, our Sunday *tiffin* their farewell. We tried curry last Sunday and the cook made it very nicely. Reid's two boys are in New Zealand, so they are bound there – only five months leave including voyages. I know where to hand over sewing-machine if we get moved. She prefers it to be used than just lying away maybe rusting.

Ian's letters are jolly good now for his age. Of course, he is at a more civilised age. Are you sure Dorothy and her father really don't mind having you two precious ones with them? Know they will like Margaret having the company, but think it must often be trying for you. Know they are very very kind and have been terribly good to us all but I know it can't always be easy. Of course these war days everyone's lives are upset and different. It would be harder for them if they had evacuees billeted on them. Carrick seems lucky that way. How does money go these days? Are you managing comfortably enough?

18 November.
To Gran from Mummy. What a busy time we have had with such a spate of meals in our own house. Budge and Howard and a Belgian friend from Singapore came on Saturday for tea, then we watched a rugger match and sat at Club with others and had quite a nice time until 9.30 then home for dinner and they left about twelve. This Belgian has two very big sons at school in Brastagi [the Cameron

Highlands equivalent in Sumatra], her husband is Dutch but she divorced him years ago and works in Singapore. She is very nice and enjoyed everything. I think we are such a homely family that certain people find us a complete change, so quiet and contented and happy. There are so many mess-ups in families in this country. Klang seems like the wilds compared to busy, enormous Singpore. Howard is keen on gardening and very jolly and nice in a quiet way. It was a cheery night and a good meal and the attractive, cheap Japanese dishes always amuse people.

On Sunday we went to Church and brought the padre and another young padre, a soldier who played the harmonium, home for *tiffin*: curry and rice, beef, prawns, vegetables and then rice pudding. The visiting padre stayed on and got a bed to sleep in, which was a treat he said, after camping so long. Not that he was in bed very long. We had tea fairly early as he was preaching in the Methodist Church at six o'clock. After tea we showed him Klang and dropped him at his kirk! He enjoyed eating all the new kinds of fruit and had never tasted curry so all a change and profuse thanks! Then last night two young men and the Welfare Centre nurse (a Miss Clark), had dinner with us. She is quiet and very different from most females in the east. I meet her a lot at the knitting parties and sometimes in the Club. Wallace brought a Siamese cat for her (he has a puppy and the cat didn't get on with it and she wanted another cat). Both crazy about animals, worse than we are even. I'd been out in the morning to Bree's at Port Swettenham and she took puppies and I took our cat, to vet down there, so our puss now has a strapping on a hip she damaged two weeks ago. Friday I was riding at Speedins, so you see how the time flies. Mrs Reid and a new Mrs Falconer are coming here this morning and I've to run the knitting party for a few weeks so little spare time. Billie got tennis yesterday but pouring rain today again; nearly every day wet lately. David is looking so boyish with tiny wee rompers instead of nappy. A friend has eight attractive puppies. We'd like one but hopeless in a flat and perhaps best not till David is older. Shirley Jane is enough to be going on with.

20 November
Everyone waiting these days to see what Japan is going to do and yet no one seems at all concerned, because it's nothing new, we've been waiting and watching Japan for years now but surely that must be settled one way or the other soon. It doesn't seem possible to keep peace in the Pacific and yet nothing is surprising nowadays. I expect the news at this end has been worrying you but I do hope not much. Of course we'd cable if there was any big news. In many ways you are better in quiet Carrick than in Dollar. When he goes back to school there we want him to be a day boy. Am sure the food problem is easier for you in Carrick [not many now will recall wartime rationing]. Hope our parcels reach you all right; feel afraid that the second one of woollies has maybe gone west. Expect you get plenty wool for war knitting which will keep you busy and which you enjoy doing. I'm on another pullover just now. Just finished nice little skirt for evacuee.

Never have half enough time to do all I want to and yet wearying for Ham's holidays to begin. It seems ages since the term began. I'm just tired of all our separations. Billie is fine but any cold catches him in the kidneys or lumbago or whatever that bad spot of his is. Such very damp weather just now. You have no idea what a joy your letters are. David was at the Club yesterday and got some petting for a change! I was golfing and enjoyed it and had played Mah Jongg in the morning. Reids are away, Mrs brought the new Mrs D O (District Officer, that's no 1 Government servant in the district) a Mrs Falconer, a bride and

81

Australian and awfully nice. We had coffee and eats and a good chat. He was a widower so must be years older. She seems a dear, bonny too and quite tall. Mrs Reid is a wee grey mouse in looks and ways but a real good soul and I like her very much. David is getting calcium to help teeth and bones to grow. The cat is getting it as well!

20 November.
To Ian from Daddy. We get a letter from Hamish every Tuesday and he seems to be very well. He is lucky for Klang is very hot and damp just now. We get such a lot of rain that the golf course is very often under water. The Club and the golf course are nearly next the Bank so we have not got far to walk to them. It is just as well as otherwise we would have to go by car. No one walks any distance here as it is far too hot and one gets so sweaty. You will be into winter now. We could do with some of your cold weather.

Cameron Highlands 22 November.
To Mummy and Daddy from Hamish. Next week Reverend Mother is coming to test us in all our work, Numbers, Reading, Spelling, Phonics(*sic*), French and Writing. I am going to try hard to get full marks for all to make you very happy. We have had nice walks when it was fine. Thanks for the money you sent. I got a little something for you but it will be a secret till Christmas. Tons of love and kisses from Hamish [and the rest of the page another battle scene between planes (one marked 'spitfir') and ships flying swastikas, most of which are sinking. A long way from early drawings of Fuji in the sunset.]

22 November.
To Gran from Mummy. I'm in the midst of making David's big new green mosquito net. Ham's old green one has been

used all the time but is too small for playpen now that the lad stands up and staggers about so much; his cot is a light green too (belongs to Philps in K.L) and just now he has an ordinary single bed, white net, a little too big. D only sleeps there at nights; all day long in the pen. The green net had to come from Singapore; heavy duty on it coming in here, as that's Straits Settlements and this Federated Malay States. Have managed to get a few odd letters off. I must be free next month during Ham's holidays.

I've fond memories of sleeping within mosquito nets, the eerie way nets diffused the world beyond their haven, very much a place for the imagination to roam in safe freedom. They never felt claustrophobic. How inexplicable too that an insect so delicate and dainty could demand such defences. Equally recalled is the use of a Flit-gun to whoosh-whoosh into corners of the room – with a very distinctive smell.

26 November

Hamish will be back in less than 2 weeks, thank goodness. I golfed on Sunday and B played tennis on Monday, so we've had drier weather. What a busy three days – I left here at eight on Monday, to K.L. for a hair appointment at nine – washed and set, at last, well over a month since last decently done. Then had my eyes tested and then shopping and then to Howard's estate five miles away for *tiffin*. We went and saw a piggery, beautifully kept, a big pukka house with cement floor and running water and pens for the different families, hundreds of good clean pigs of all ages, some just like wee puppies. It's part of their business of course. Had a drink and a delicious *tiffin* and sat talking till four. I thought it was only three and had a fit as the eye man was making a special effort (by his way of it!) to have my glasses ready for 4.30. Got into the town about two minutes before 4.30 so collected the goggles all right. He used my red frames for dark glasses and another nice new pair, as comfy, Japanese ones were never right. It's not eyesight so much as muscles, and worse he says when run-down, causes headaches and tired feeling. I seem calm enough and dashed easy-going but suppose just strung-up a bit and I don't take things easily inwardly. Went on to Kings for tea in station hotel. Home to meet B in Club.

Nice letter from Dorothy. I do a good bit of knitting in car and at Club. Yesterday got David weighed in chemist scales (he is too wriggly for ours) and he is 24½ lbs, so that's splendid. He is going to collect money for war fund today, people guessing his weight – in Club, rugger match before and then wee dance and supper (only gramophone). Budge and Howard are coming for tea.

Collected new Mrs Falconer yesterday morning, after parking *amah* and David back home, went to McGanns for Mah Jongg and tea, quite a big party for the morning. Then knitting meeting in afternoon, a busy time and I've been rolled into going to examine a Girls School's needlework – can you imagine it? Rush home and changed and away with B to K.L. to have dinner with Hendersons, Chartered's number one. Lovely meal, Philips there too then on to a film, then a drink at Club and after one o'clock to bed. Mrs Henderson is youngish and used to work in Chartered in London. Cheery nice time although a solemn picture.

23 November.

David collected about $20 yesterday and was a huge success, especially in the men's bar after the match. He went a wee walk in the pram to get cooled down after so many people had been holding him. He loves the pram; it's a treat because he is so seldom in it. He sits there just delighted and never wriggles, such a change to see him sit still. *Amah* loves to take him to the Malay King's house, as she calls the Palace. She is very willing and pleasant and just crazy about D and very capable too. Two big raffles and the market stall (and David) brought in roughly $170 (dollars) so that was very good. Budge and Howard came all right and we had an energetic night, dancing with the soldiers, thirty of them. Half of them played rugger against the Klang district team. Mostly young, raw, Yorkshire lads but all very well behaved and appreciated the party. There are so many soldiers in this country that they can't get enough to do. It's very hard for them, but difficult for the civilians as well as they can't do very much for thousands and thousands of them. I'm quite pleased not to ride today, one horse is at the vet and Mrs Speedin has visitors. I must get David's rompers made. I gave tailor blue silk for shirt for Hamish for Xmas parties. Have to do Xmas shopping before Ham arrives. Wicker chairs for them both should please them and be useful.

Klang 27 November, 1941.
To Ian, from Daddy. Davie was a great success at the Club last night. Mummie was running the monthly market and we had a competition to guess Davie's weight. Fifty cents a chance and the prize was a big cake. We have those markets once a month for war funds and it was Mummy's turn to run it. People gave all sorts of things to sell, fruit and vegetables from all the planters' houses and then there are raffles as well. We got over £20 yesterday which was quite good. Davie was a new stunt and he was very good and smiling and laughing all the time I had him in the bar end of the Club. Hamish comes back on 7th December and we will go to K.L. to meet his train.

Cameron Highlands. 27 November.
To Mummy and Daddy, from Hamish. How quickly the days have passed. This is my last letter to you. One more week of school and then the holidays. I am longing to see you all. I am sure we are going to have a lovely time together. I have written to Santa Claus …

This would indeed be the last letter and I wonder what happened to the school after the 'lovely' time turned into nightmare. Japanese forces invaded neutral Siam (we wouldn't for defence purposes) and Malaya, on the very day I arrived home from school, 7th December 1941, K.L. and Port Swettenham would fall on January 12, and Singapore on February 15. (7 December was also the date for the attack on Pearl Harbor.)

As was customary I had been sent up to the Cameron Highlands to the Convent School there so as to enjoy the better climate. The Cameron Highlands is the country's most extensive hill station and takes its name from the Government surveyor who came across it in 1885 but who did not name it on maps, so it was only in 1925, when a senior civil servant realised its potential (as he'd seen at Fraser's Hill, 75km north of K.L.) that it rapidly developed. Fraser of Fraser's Hill (a lesser hill station) had worked in the Australian gold rush, then came to Malaya in the 1890s, found tin in 'them thar hills' and set to work. After 25 years he disappeared and it was a search party in 1917 which fully realised that here was a place to escape the stifling heat and humidity of K.L. or Singapore (which lies just over one degree north of the equator).

The Cameron Highlands would see tea planters arriving from India, Chinese cultivating vegetable farms, hoteliers building for holiday takers, and the rich setting up their 'castles in the air'. The climate is generally wet and cloudy, but that produces the many shades of green, the good waterfalls and an astonishing flora. A few villages lie along the tortuous road through the mountains with Tanah Rata the principal settlement, and the site of the Pensionnat Notre Dame, my school. The main tea growing area is five kilometres south, at Ringlet, and long after father had retired, a miniature tea chest arrived each year from the Boh Tea Estate, one of the local estates. On mother's visit we went for long walks by the river and enjoyed visits to the Green Cow, a tearoom, the name never to be forgotten, and used decades on in a short story I wrote.

I do recall the school uniform: purply-coloured shirts and grey shorts. Quantities were laid down: 4 shirts, 3 trousers, 6 socks and so on – and all had to have Cash's name tapes sewn onto them. My memories of the school itself are almost non-existent. Some of the buildings were built up off the ground and of course finding access to these subterranean areas appealed to boys; places to be explored, to be claimed as dens. (I hate to think what other, possibly venomous, creepy crawlies and slithery things lived there.) As mentioned, I did have a spell in the isolation ward on contracting ringworm and had to endure the embarrassment of my head being shaved and bright purple permanganate applied to the spots.

At school there was a craze for marbles and I delighted not only in the fierce competition but in the marbles themselves, those smooth, clear globes shot through with rainbow colours. Magic. We collected them avidly as much as playing with them (status according to the size of one's hoard?) and hated being beaten which meant losing one. There were two games: one involved a 'cup' (as in golf), the object to hole out I presume (the rules are long forgotten), the other the vicious thumb-flicking of a marble missile to hit an opponent's out of a circle drawn on the ground. I wonder what the nuns thought of our warlike yells of glee and bitter screams of loss.

Over the years I've often wondered where and when I began to read and write. I've no memory of the process but seeing my Malay letters it was clearly at the Pensionnat Notre Dame under the kindly tutelage of the sisters; kindly, or I'm sure I would remember. An early letter survives because mother filled up the rest of the space writing to Ian, commenting, 'the drawing on the other side is better than the effort at a letter, isn't it?' That drawing is of a British battleship firing off guns with two planes overhead. *Every letter* was to have war scenes on them which, through 1941, became increasingly violent battle scenes, often between swastika-flying ships and our planes, an irony with what was to come with the sinking by Japanese planes of the British warships, the *Repulse* and *Prince of Wales*.

I presume I heard about the war at far away 'home' from adult gossip, Newsreels – and comics! No doubt there were things I was not supposed to hear about. Anyway, there was this bloodthirsty boy who loved drawing battles. When I eventually reached Scotland a few years later and was asked what I wanted to be when I grew up my answer, I'm told, was 'a man who stops wars'.

As part of the learning to read and write the letters home to Klang were a weekly lesson, then corrected, and written out in copybook hand; a painless enough exercise so that I don't remember any of it. So, thank you, sisters at Notre Dame. I don't think there was much attempt at proselytizing their charges though I do remember saying, after David game me a kick when I leaned over him 'Mummy, David has just kicked me in Jesus.'

88

6

Klang, In Sorrow

Carrick Castle, 4 December 1941.
To Hamish from Ian. A week or two ago Gran and I went up to Glasgow for the weekend. We were at the Simpsons'. John and I had a good time on Sunday. John is Mr Simpson's grandson and we are good friends. On Monday Gran and I did our shopping and we came back on Tuesday. At school there are fifteen pupils, which is a record. The school will have a new teacher after the Xmas holiday for Miss Livingstone is leaving. It will be four years in May since we were together. Of the pair of mitts, I have finished one and have done up to the thumb of the second.

December 5
At school there was a Grammar test, including Dictation and I was first. I had 77%, William Boyd 72%, Margaret 65%, Hamish 63%, Andy 62% and Ina Durham had 6% and Archie McLeod had 1%. Wasn't that awful? I had 9 ½ out of 10 for Dictation. I think I am improving at school.

Klang 6 December
To Gran from Mummy. We are looking forward to meeting Hamish tomorrow. Just couldn't find him a 'tommy gun,' one of his requests to Santa Claus. Not a decent gun to be

had. No choice of toys in the shops and what a price, ditto balloons and crackers. I got three dozen of each, for David's birthday, any left over would do Xmas but haven't ordered any Xmas food or anything yet. Ditto with a wee Xmas tree and odds and ends. No use risking getting unnecessary things just now. Got Ham a real football, small size, also good new sandals. Had to get his things before he came, as he'll be with me any other time in K.L. before Xmas. David's rocker chair in shape of a hen is lovely, ditto his wee wicker feeding chair. Going to have tea with Peacocks in Kuala Lumpur, before collecting Hamish from the train. They have a wee boy just a little younger than David.

Klang. 6 December.
To Ian. From Daddy. I am very busy in the office at present as Miller my assistant has been mobilised and I am now on my own. He is in the armoured cars. We are all wondering what the Japs are going to do. They will get a very warm reception if they tackle this country for we are well prepared and more so now that the fleet has arrived at Singapore. It was a surprise to see that the *Prince of Wales* had arrived there. Hamish will be home tomorrow and we will go up to K.L. to meet him. We got a lot of letters this week and I hope ours are reaching you safely.
All the best, biggest son.

This was written the day before Pearl Harbour and the invasion of Malaya and I'm sure reflects what people felt at the time – however unbelievable with hindsight. What was about to happen was what was inconceivable to everyone out in Malaya. The *Prince of Wales* and the *Repulse* were sunk just a few days later, attacked by 85 well-trained strike aircraft. So much for the belief that planes couldn't sink ships and Japanese pilots were quite ineffective.

Carrick Castle. 8 December.

To Hamish from Ian. At school I got 77 out of 100 for Grammar and I was first as well. Arithmetic is my best and favourite subject. What is your favourite subject? How is Peter? Is he growing into a nice cat? The cat Aunt Dorothy had died a good time ago. I have over 1500 stamps in my collection. I have been collecting for two years. Have you got a special friend at school? At Dollar, before Carrick, my special friend was a boy I knew in Ceylon, Jimmie Galbraith.

We are wondering if you are all still in Klang with all this trouble going on. You may have been evacuated. I hope you are alright. I do not know if Gran and I are going to town during the Christmas holidays. I wish the war was over and we were all together. Gran is very kind and so is Aunt Dorothy but Gran is kinder by a long shot and not so ratty.

8 December.

To Ian from Mummy. We are now sampling our very first real black-out. Daddy is in the ARP here, doing his shift from 5 till 1, but he got home at 6.30 for a quick meal, Hamish loves having his supper with us as usually we are much later. He went off to bed singing after his first day at home. We met him in K.L. last night all right and he looks nice and pink and fit, has grown a lot and is full of energy. We had tea with some friends in K.L. before going to collect the lad at the train.

So at last Japan is actually at war with us so now we feel a bit more like you people at home. We are all very well and hope you are too. You will be into real winter. You are lucky to be cool, here we are much too hot. There are no changes in the seasons like Bangkok even, always very much the same heat with rain any time.

I have been busy making blackout curtains from coloured bed-covers, even that's not long enough, have to join other curtains or anything, we have such enormous windows and dozens of rings to sew on as they must be able to pull in the day time.

Had a crowd of visitors yesterday, some young ones for Ham. Busy making arrangements for David's birthday (ordered cake today) and have had so much telephoning to do. We are going to decorate the cake ourselves, with candle in middle in fancy holder and wee flags with all the children's names on them. Ham is delighted with this idea.

What a lot seems to have happened since the beginning of this scrawl! Now we are in the same position as you dear ones and hope you aren't too worried. Really just as well you didn't manage to join us, Ian's schooling would have been even more upset here than where he is, as well as all the risky journey to be in just as dangerous a place and worse climate. We are all outrageously fit and bright and long before this gets to you, we'll cable. May wait for a Xmas greetings one. Please don't be worried, so far we are very comfy, remember London and Dollar is something like Singapore and Klang for distances apart (and roughly same differences in sizes). At last we know definitely where we are with the Japs. The treacherous beginning of it was so typical of them; expect they think they are mighty smart. The strain of waiting is over now which is something definite. We are busy enough not to feel that waiting feeling so much, although there is a mighty lot we'll have to wait long enough for.

Hamish is now busy writing your letter, entirely on his own. He is terribly pleased with everything and is an active little goat. He loves helping me to make wee flags to decorate Davie's birthday cake; ordered it this morning. To help make the enormous curtains for the blackout I have used our new fairly dark blue cotton bedcovers with some curtains joined to them. Tried to write the other night but blackout light much too bad. It was first time B was away from five until one in the morning. It felt quite exciting.

Daddy is on duty at ARP headquarters every second night at that time. I'll send a wee meal round to him now. He is settled to that definite war job. He is terribly busy in the office as Miller is away being a real soldier. B also arranges shifts for the different men fire-watching in turns, ditto the servants, so everyone is busy. I've to reassure the *amah*, naturally she is worried about family in Hong Kong. Mrs Waite came from Carey Island [off Port Swettenham] where her husband is manager of a big rubber estate. Her daughter was to be married, huge wedding in K.L., but soldier fiancé suddenly had to go off to Kota Baru in the north and she went to marry him there (just registry office), parents and sister went with her, terrible tiring journey. Waites were newly back home when the news came [of the Jap invasion] and now the bride is back, evacuated exactly one week after the wedding. You hear of personal family affairs much worse than our own, don't you?

Some children came to play with Ham and a bunch of women here for tea and Mah Jongg so it was a full house. Weans here in evening, after Ham had been playing with Pamela Sharp at Club. He has more company this holiday, several new people with weans. Felt less like Xmas and birthday preparations last year, not knowing what was what, but now we just must carry on for children as normally as possible. No inclination, time, or opportunity for any adult parties. We just say *tid' apa* [no matter/so be it] and get on with things. We must try to encourage Ham to keep up his drawing, he is so quick and good. Reading, writing, spelling and sums have all improved greatly, he has done splendidly this term at school. Next week I plan to pack some breakables away as the barer the house the better for blackouts, easier to move about in, and less work for everyone. Have just had lovely new stands made for the plants and they are getting painted now. The boy-syce has been making them himself; he's a gem. Look after yourselves well and thanks again and again for all your goodness to Ian.

12 December.
To Ian, from Daddy. What a lot seems to have happened since last week. The very morning we met Hamish in Kuala Lumpur we were at war with Japan. We are blacked out every night now but so far that is our only inconvenience. My only assistant in the Bank, Miller, is mobilised and has gone to join his unit, the armoured cars. I am the only European left in the office but the native staff (Chinese) have carried on spectacularly and everything is going smoothly.

I am on ARP duty, 1 am to 9am tonight, so I will have to go to bed early and get some sleep. Nothing happening here and we are about as far away from the North as the South so nothing much should happen.

14 December.
To Gran from Mummy. A wee scrawl written at the Club where Hamish has been playing since tea time and we are just about to go home for our blackout meal. Saw a lovely Diana Durban film last night and Ham and the *amah* went to the matinee. Billie's one free night lately, now he is in ARP headquarters and this morning had a rushed run to K.L. to do with Bank. Ham went with him, while I got some odd jobs done, made cloth braces to tie David to his chairs and pram (simply could not get leather ones anywhere) and these are much cooler and softer and quite strong.

Now is Wednesday 17th and we've just had two of the very busiest days running. B terribly busy in office and often out doing his ARP shift. David's birthday party kept me busy: at last minute our order for cakes and fancy bread was cancelled, so had to get everything done at home, all quite successful but quite a rush. Ten weans had a lovely time, good tea and crackers, then playing with balloons, then ice-cream, more play, then off home, each with a big balloon. Davie got some nice presents, a blue pusher and spoon, adorable blue egg cup and spoon, very cute feeder, a big soft ball, $5 (dollars which is 11/8d), a rattle, a tooth brush in attractive holder and Hamish got a lovely Meccano set and he was very proud and delighted with everything. He had a boy, same age, his best pal at school, spending the whole day with him and his mother fetched him at night. Nearly all the other weans had mothers and *amahs* for tea too so it was some house, then fathers later on for drinks. A very full day.

Next morning had women whose husbands are all soldiers for tea and Mah Jongg in morning, one had her daughter of thirteen so again Ham had company and ice-cream, etc! That same evening we sent our pair out to friends on a rubber estate, Gray, (elderly couple) to stay with them, priceless packing the car with all their *barang* [stuff/belongings]. In between times I have been overhauling clothes for evacuees, so really haven't had a spare minute. Now this morning I went to Grays' for our usual weekly Mah Jongg and tea which I'd likely have called off if our weans hadn't been staying there. They are settling down beautifully, very fit and happy. We are all quite comfy meantime, so hope you aren't worrying. Must write shorter letters but mean to cable you tomorrow. Think you are waiting to make the monthly one the Xmas one. Do hope Ian is getting on with the Dalton plan. Suppose you had better try and get him back to Dollar, as a day pupil, and want you to be together anyhow - even if he'd to travel from Dunfermline; he is big enough now for that if it was the only way. Expect you are like ourselves, doing a lot of listening to radio news. What a world mess but it will all get tidied up some day. Everyone keeps cheery. Now, previous one, will leave this scrap for B – not supposed to write long letters now.

Dear Gran,
All well and happy here. Don't worry about us. Am very busy but otherwise normal. Effie very busy too. All the best, Billie.

Klang 17 December.
To Ian, from Mummy. David had a lovely birthday: ten children and all had a splendid time. We only wanted you beside them, but you would have been older than any other. Maureen Oliver is 10½, her brother 8½ then Ham's best school friend Kenneth Paton, 7½, same as Ham. Pamela Sharp is 6, Rosemary and Elizabeth Miller are 4 and 5, then Vanessa Speedin and David Bree are both 2½, the lad of the day 1, so wasn't that a good selection of steps and stairs? They had a lovely tea. We decorated the cake with meringues with flags with each one's name and the candle in centre (a fairly big one). Crackers and balloons, ice-cream and lemonade and it was time to go home so we couldn't show the film. Such a lot of mothers, fathers, *amahs* so we had a crowded flat and a busy time, all very successful. He got some lovely little presents. Hamish helped me to decorate the dining room with old decorations we had. They're still up and yet the wee lads are both away spending a while on a rubber estate with friends. I saw them this morning.

Kenneth Paton, my 'best friend' would also reach Dollar, their home on the Back Road, ours on the Muckhart Road (with writer George Blake next door) and we all went to Dollar Academy, Kenneth to become Head Boy (1951-52) and go on to a distinguished medical career which would end tragically in 1990 (just two years before retiring) when he and another consultant at Pinderfields Hospital, near Wakefield, were savagely attacked and killed by a fanatical Iraqi inmate who, many years later was found dead in the secure hospital where he was held. The family managed to escape Malaya (on 1 February, on a troopship which had just disembarked the 18th Division – only to soon be in Japanese hands), but Kenneth's father ended as a POW of the Japanese, experiencing the horrors of Singapore's Changi gaol, and two uncles were also interned.

Carrick Castle. 18 December.
To Mummy and Daddy, from Ian. On Tuesday as Andy, Hamish and I had no knitting, Andy and I cleaned and tidied 3 shelves of the cupboard, then this afternoon Hamish and I cleaned 7 shelves. On Tuesday we did the worst shelves; they were for the silent reading books and we had to put them in the order of the author's first letter. Miss Livingstone gave me a book called *By Ship and Plane to the Pole* and a few short stories. It is a very good book. I got it on Monday and finished it on Wednesday. We have had no snow so far. Aunt Dorothy went away on Wednesday on the *Comet* to see friends.

Klang 21 December 1941
To Gran, from Mummy. The two lads and Mr and Mrs Gray came and had tea with us here yesterday, Hamish was very thrilled. He is having lovely walks with Gray every morning at the rubber estate and was telling us all about

the different grades of trees and how they grew and how they were 'rubbered'. What a chatterbox and really quite smart, and Mrs G is very pleased with the way he eats and goes off to bed and never a grumble, and is very jolly. Mind you, with folks he doesn't like he can be a terror! They have two grown up daughters, one in Greenock now and another daughter in Australia at school, and really seem to like having the young company and are sensible and wouldn't be soft. *Amah* is good with the small one and attends to all his food, so he is no trouble and is in his pen nearly all day long, he laughs so easily.

I've been packing our china and pictures and linen etc. Odd cloth makes such good packing. Before coming here from Japan I packed the breakables all through our clothes and it was very successful, but can't do that this time. B has never before been quite so busy in a Bank (and that's going some) and then out at ARP alternate nights, gives very little sleep compared to normal but these certainly aren't normal times. Hope you get our Xmas cables, send in plenty time we thought. Not able to post parcels now, and I'd got to the length of sleeves in your striped jersey. Nothing like that really matters now. Material things won't matter much after the war. We personally have never fussed about them much but lots of folks will change their ideas of values, drastically. So far, think you have had a peaceful time lately. Wonder if the Germans will try more blitzing of Britain after their Russian fiasco. News also of Libya, has been splendid lately. Excuse scrap, terribly busy but we are doing away fine.

I've quite clear memories of various visits to rubber estates and was fascinated by the way the trees were tapped. I loved watching the men quietly working, paring down the cuts, so sap flowed to a small metal lip from which the creamy latex dropped into a tin or half coconut. I forget where but on one occasion I managed to scare myself thoroughly. Any rubber cultivation was simply an oasis in the green, overpowering fecundity of jungle which presented almost a wall into which I forced my inquisitive way. In a very few yards I felt as if swallowed up in a terrifying, choking, greenery. I could still see the sun flickering through the fret of trees, and I fought in rising panic to escape back to the open. Give me honest desert any day.

Some envelopes of letters from Malaya have also survived, all opened and resealed, marked *Passed by censor* or *Passed for transmission* (the innocent-looking ones to 'Master Ian Brown'). There is one in an envelope of the Adelphi Hotel, Singapore, franked 22.2.41 so is from our first few days in the country. The other two are in Klang bank envelopes with the stamp showing the notable mosque at K.L.

Letters to Malaya are much more interesting. Two are stamped *No Service. Return to Sender*, which was back to Ian at Carrick, with one (with a London mark of 15.12.42) readdressed to 11 Station Road, Dollar (where Gran and Ian had moved for Ian returning to Dollar schooling and where we would eventually all be united).

One really does tell a story; ten months in all. It is franked Lochgoilhead 31.10.41 but then ran into the *No Service. Return to Sender*. (It was too late for a Klang delivery). But this one bears another stamp saying *Damaged by Sea Water*, which is fairly obvious as stained and the stamp had floated off, and it had been *Officially Sealed* once again. The inference is that the ship carrying this mail was either sunk or damaged, with the mail rescued after the immersion. It was franked 8.8.42, then Lochgoilhead on 10.8.42 only to be readdressed from Carrick to Dunfermline (Aunt Iza's address). London - Carrick in two days in wartime seems creditable.

Later mother would use space on a notelet for 'Baby's first Christmas' to summarise our movements, which were so sudden that they were only reported home after reaching Singapore.

24 Dec. Grays and Ham visited Klang, left 12:30. I went for them. Two alerts on way back. Shelter on roadside. No lunch. Left Klang 3pm, sailed from Port Swettenham 5pm. Anchored half mile out, loading. 25 Dec 2 o'clock came back. Raid. Telephone B, he collected us, home Klang 4pm. B had turkey party *tiffin*. Went to Falconers for Xmas dinner and walked home. 26 Dec. Packing. Bad air raid. No lunch. Hunt in garden for Ham. Sailed from Port Swettenham about 4pm on wee ship *Ipoh*. 500 Jap internees in the hold. Malay and Australian guards. Captain Mackie doing conjuring tricks. 27 Dec Singapore – Seaview hotel. At dinner, from door across the large busy dining room, half-naked Hamish's 'Mummie, David's yelling!'

The Seaview was one of Singapore's best. A postcard survives showing its over-furnished Reading and Music Room. Obviously services were being maintained despite ever more raids. No doubt it was filled with displaced families, all doing what they were ordered, as well-disciplined Brits.

I don't recall being particularly frightened during raids. On one occasion in Klang I had to be fetched from the bank's flat roof as I thought I'd have a much better view from there. The noise was always terrific – and the fires. It would be even worse in Singapore with its huge buildings or wooden areas, going up like giant torches, crackling and roaring, a very particular sound, so deeply set in my unconscious that when forty years on I woke from sleep hearing the sound again, the hairs on my neck rose in horror. Fire! An inferno. But in Burntisland? I quickly put on my *djellaba* dressing gown and went out onto the road. Three hundred yards along the way a garage was burning, the similarity to Singapore the more marked as petrol in cans or cars periodically exploded. How to describe the sound? It was a bit like the sound of the cereal that goes 'crackle and pop' when milk is poured on – multiplied a thousandfold. Strangely no other neighbour appeared. They didn't hear it. But they had not been in Singapore.

I carry a permanent reminder of these days in a ganglion on my knee the size of half a golf ball. I was hit by a minute flying fragment during a raid in either Klang or Singapore which, no doubt, would be given a dab of iodine and have a plaster put on it (what boy's knees are not always being scarred?) Later, it was just possible to see a little black speck under the skin. I was not averse to flaunting this to classmates in South Africa or Scotland. My war wound! Alas, over the years the ganglion grew over the spot and now nothing can be seen. The lump did help me on one adult occasion to win a knobbly knees competition.

Two last letters from Singapore are very different from the chatty ones of a month before. Klang obviously had to be abandoned in haste. It seems astonishing how little was reported home of what was happening and how much continued as before. Mother was playing Mah Jongg on the 17th and on Christmas Day we were aboard a ship trying to escape. K.L. fell on January 11.

Sea View Hotel, Singapore. 30 December 1941.
To Gran and Ian from Mummy. Here we are on our travels once again. I wish B was with us but of course quite impossible. Things will improve someday soon. All very rushed and sudden but all serene and chins well up. Don't worry

if no letters for some time. Cabled and did lots of things today, Bank people frantically busy but a great help to us.

No time for more, keep smiling and best love
ever your loving
Effie xx

This last letter must have been left to be posted, as mother and we two boys sailed from Singapore on 1 January, the dating a slip no doubt. It was scribbled in pencil.

2 January 1942.
My dearest Mummie and Ian. Want to take this opportunity of posting, although there has been really no time to write. Please tell Iza, Aunts Effie, Nellie, Bess etc that it is almost impossible to write and pass on our news such as it is and love to everyone, especially Dorothy. Glad to think of you precious ones being with her and now events have proved it was a good thing you didn't get into Malaya. Hope we'll meet in a more comfortable spot, some day fairly soon. Hate being away from B but no doubt of what had to be done – taking the weans away. All very sudden and many folks in much worse predicaments! Hope you are all well and comfy. Please give my love to all pals and explain impossibility of writing letters, simply no time and goodness knows when this will reach you but you would get the cable and understand.

Keep cheery and look after your precious selves.
Bestest love and heaps of it.
Effie xx

We sailed on a Dutch liner, NV *Marnix van St Aldegonde* (named after Philip of Marnix, Lord of Sainte-Aldegonde, one of the heroes of the Dutch Wars of Independence). We travelled with a troopship *Orion*, heading to Australia, and escorted by two destroyers, *Tenedos* and *Thanet* as far as the Sunda Strait. The troopship rather points to Australian forces being disembarked at Singapore, as many were, far too late and ill-equipped to stop the Japanese rush down Malaya. The Japs were nearing Klang and K.L. at this stage. The *Tenedos* was later sunk by the enemy off Ceylon and the main base in Ceylon, Trincomalee, suffered a Pearl Harbour-style raid from aircraft carrier forces that left 12 of 18 aircraft destroyed on the ground. We reached Durban on 19 January 1942.

History, however, is the record of mistakes and Japan's vast fanning out of forces with such extended supply lines, running from the edge of India and Ceylon, to Australia and through much of the Pacific was a miscalculation. Wanting to 'rule the world' has always been doomed: Alexander, the Mongols, Romans, Arabs, Napoleon, British, Hitler, Japan had to fail eventually. The price has always been the bloody misery of millions. History is hell and the world is still struggling to find any present heaven on earth.

7

Father's Story

Carrick Castle, 18 January 1942.
To Daddy from Ian I hope you are all right. We had a
postcard from Aunt Iza a few days ago saying she had had
a letter from the Bank saying that the staff from Klang and
Kuala Lumpur were safe and well at Singapore. Gran and
I are both very well but still anxious about you all but I
should think Mummy and two brothers will be out of the
danger zone. I am wearing Mummy's grey pullover and it
is very warm. Mr and Mrs MacLean came yesterday and
I was showing Mrs MacLean some of Hamish's drawings
and letters and a photo of David. Mrs Maclean said Hamish's drawings and letters were very good.

Gran used up the rest of the space telling about her and Aunt
Iza's efforts to get information out of the bank in London.
They could only report father had reached Singapore and
the family planned to go to South Africa. Should she and
Ian try and find passages to join them? That however was
out of the question. It would take two years for us to leave
South Africa! How disjointed the times were. The next
letter from Father to Ian, on the 19th, would be old news
before Ian's of the 18th would arrive.

Adelphi Hotel, Singapore, 19 January 1942.

To Ian, from Daddy. What a lot has happened since last I wrote to you. I left Klang on the night of the 4th, had two days in Kuala Lumpur and then came on here by car on the 7th. It was not a bit too soon as the Japs were in both places very soon after. You would get Mummie's wire saying that she had sailed [for South Africa] and to address her care of Uncle Jim. She should be there now and I am just waiting on a wire to say they have arrived. Cables are taking a very long time to come these days, one from London for the Bank took nearly a month. Hope I get mine soon now. I got the one from Carrick the other day and was glad to know you were all well. Singapore is a very big busy place after Klang. All the Malayan branches of the Bank are in the building of the Yokohama Specie Bank and as there are eight branches it is a bit of a squash. Singapore seems to get quite a lot of raids. The day the family left Klang we had quite a bad raid and some bombs just outside the office. We were all downstairs in a fine safe place but the poor flat upstairs was a nasty mess especially when it rained as bits of tiles had been blown off. I was glad that Mummie and the boys got away safely so soon after that. Hamish was very brave and after the planes had gone he was very busy taking water to the wounded men. Some were brought into the office until the ambulance came for them. Davie cried while the raid was going on but just for a minute or two and then he was all right. You have two brave young brothers. Hamish could not be found when the alarm went but fortunately a man saw him and brought him inside.

We are very busy in the office but how pleasant most people are to see the Bank and know that they have their money even if they have lost everything else. Mummie took a lot of my things away when she came and I also brought a lot here so compared with most people we have been very lucky. Lots have lost everything except the clothes they were in. Well, must stop my boy, don't worry about me, I am all right.

Hope you are all well.

Love from Daddy.

Our first week on reaching Singapore had been spent in the Adelphi Hotel so the same hotel seeing father's last days had a certain roundness to it.

Father was to record his experiences later on (in South Africa and/or Madras) and these follow, in chronological order: 'Exit Klang' (and a note on falling bombs); 'Kuala Lumpur to Singapore'; 'Singapore and Afterwards'.

Exit Klang

When Japan entered the war I was stationed in Klang which is 4¾ miles from Port Swettenham [now Port Klang] and about 25 from Kuala Lumpur. It is the centre of an important rubber district and although there were few Europeans in the town a considerable number were within a distance of a few miles. From a strategic viewpoint Klang is of no small importance as it is the site of a bridge over the Klang River, about 250 ft wide at this point, and also the junction of four main roads to: - (1) Kuala Lumpur (2) Port Swettenham (3) Kuala Selangor and (4) Port Dickson and Malacca (via Banting). It was therefore to be expected that the Japs would give it early attention.

My only European Assistant, R.D. (Ginger) Miller, being in the Armoured Car Section of the FMS [Federated Malang States] Volunteers, had already gone but with the help of our two local assistants we were able to get along comfortably for a time. We were kept very busy but as we closed at 1 o'clock each day we were not too hard pressed.

I was doing duty in the ARP Control room and as I could not undertake to be there during the day I was on continuous night duty, eight hour spells either from 5pm to 1am, or from 1am to 9am. Headquarters was the Malay Boys School only a short distance from the Office and I had my dinner sent along to me each evening when I was on duty.

We had our ARP organisation in the Bank as well and all arrangements worked very well to begin with. All the staff were very keen and the plants on the roof garden outside my flat were never kept so well watered in their existence. Stirrup pumps are really first rate for this.

Until 26th December things went along normally; we had occasional alarms and Jap planes came and had a look see either at Klang or Port Swettenham almost daily. There was at that time absolutely no defence against them; the nearest aerodrome was at Kuala Lumpur where they had a few Brewster Buffaloes said to be very manoeuvrable but as things turned out about 40 miles per hour slower than the Jap bombers. When a Brewster started to chase a bomber, the latter usually put on a spurt, circled round and in the end was chasing the Buffalo. That was our air defence in Malaya until a few days before the fall of Singapore when a few Hurricanes arrived, much too late. [This comment on the planes was cut from the published account.]

About 20th December the port and shipping at Port Swettenham received some attention, bombs being dropped but surprising little damage was done. They tried to get an oil tanker which was discharging but only succeeded in hitting and setting fire to the pipeline to the tanks. The fire was very soon under control. Unfortunately some of the officers of the ship jumped overboard, got stuck in the mud and were killed when a bomb landed beside them. Had they stayed on the ship they would have been safe.

My family was with me and it was not very pleasant to get up during the night and go down to our funk hole when the sirens went. My small boy of 7 was most indignant when they came and disturbed his young brother 'and on his birthday too'. [David's first birthday]

The feeling of nervousness among the staff was becoming more and more evident and our ARP organisation was getting a bit shaky. Roof spotting had to be stopped as they would not go up when an alarm went. As there were no anti-aircraft guns they were safer on the roof than anywhere else but they would not realise that and preferred to be in their *tiffin* room with only a tiled roof over them. They even left the safety of the office building and went there when we were bombed on 26th December. It was fortunate that the nearest bombs were on the other side of the building. That day, 26th December, was Klang's Waterloo for from that day it ceased to exist as an organised community.

The raid actually took place at 10.40am and we had ample warning to enable us to get all the cash and books into the safe and locked up. That part of our organisation worked splendidly and everything was in order within three minutes.

The Bank was protected by a wooden barricade (a bunding) consisting of two partitions 18' apart, the space between being filled with sand. This gave the office practically 100% protection, the only damage being ink bottles knocked over and a few panes in a glass partition broken. The planes came from south east and the first bombs were dropped on the outskirts of the town and thence in three straight lines right across the main section. The ARP Headquarters was totally wrecked, getting two direct hits and about six near misses.

The Bank was in the direct line of fire and although we escaped a direct hit the nearest bomb burst about five yards from the door to the upstairs flat in the north east corner of the building, and many others within a distance of 50 yards. The Government offices which are just opposite the Bank had a wonderful escape, three bombs bursting just short of the building and three just beyond. They had no protection and the blast did so much damage that they had to move their offices. I do not think anyone was killed but there were many injuries. My wife, two children, Dan Nicolson (a brother of Nicolson of the National Bank of India) and I were in one heap on the floor while the bombing was going on and beyond a shaking were none the worse for our experience. It was all over in no time but the noise and the trembling of the building was very alarming while it lasted. After a corpse reviver, business was resumed and carried on until the normal closing hour. Naturally there was not much doing but I was very pleased to see all the staff back on their jobs so quickly. Two large fires were blazing, one just behind R E Mohamed Kassim's shop and the crackling of the flames was clearly audible from the Bank. It says a great deal for the AFS that both fires were quickly brought under control.

In the afternoon I had a look round at the damage done and what struck me was how localised all the destruction was. Where the bombs actually struck there was considerable effect but except for the two fires mentioned the damage was very circumscribed. The flats above the office were badly knocked about, the north side one practically a wreck. Window frames and doors were blown in and there was scarcely a piece of plaster left on the walls. Glass and everything breakable had gone but strange to say my radio, which was in the middle of it all, was not even scratched. A number of tiles were blown off the roof but I did not discover this until I had to change my bedroom somewhat hurriedly to avoid being drowned. The only other building which had a protective barrier like ours was the shop of R E Mohamed Kassim & Co. Theirs looked exactly like ours but, whether to save money or not I do not know, they had omitted the very necessary filling of sand. This was very unfortunate for them as two bombs burst just outside and the bunding was blown right through the shop window where it reposed at a drunken angle with wreaths of Christmas crackers round its brow.

Among other buildings damaged was the Post Office, the Postmaster being wounded and his No. 2 killed, and from then onwards we were more or less cut off from the outside world. All wires were down and no telegrams could be sent or received for some days. The Post Office eventually moved to a house on the Batu Tiga road and the Europeans from the Customs House in Port Swettenham gallantly stepped into the breach and took the outward mails up to Kuala Lumpur in their cars and brought the inward mail back with them.

From the date of that raid Klang, as a business community, ceased to exist. All shops closed and most of the inhabitants disappeared. I went down to the office as usual next morning but no staff had turned up and I was left in the air. Shortly after a deputation appeared and said that the staff were afraid to come to the office in the mornings (all the alarms so far have been before midday) but that they would come in the afternoons instead. I had to agree and as that day was Saturday it was arranged to open on the Monday afternoon for two hours. As luck would have it we had alarms that afternoon and Port Swettenham was bombed on Sunday afternoon. This upset the apple cart again and I was then informed that the Bank being the most prominent building in Klang was bound to get it sooner or later and the staff could not work there any longer. They wanted to move out of town and I had to agree although I

110

told them they would have to work on the Monday afternoon as we had already intimated that we would be open then and I had also to try and make arrangements for a move. Monday afternoon was fortunately quiet.

After hours I had to scout round to try and find a new office and was very fortunate in finding a place about two miles from Klang. I arranged to move furniture etc next morning but when the time came no staff turned up to help with the move and no transport was available. Things appeared to have come to a standstill. However I still had a shot in my locker and I stopped an RAF lorry and asked the driver if he would like to earn $10.00 and 'Sure I would' was the reply. Well we got busy and heaped chairs, tables, typewriters etc into his lorry and got things along to our country office. Most of the staff were there so I left them to sort things out and went back to the office, found the cashier there, got the cash out and along to our new office. We had a hectic two hours making up and paying out workers' pay to planters but things on the whole went very well.

That was the last day on which things did go well. Jap planes started new tactics, coming down low over the rubber and machine-gunning anything they saw. Each day saw fewer of the staff appear until finally on the 3rd January only one ledger keeper turned up. I had a scout round and managed to collect one cashier so the three of us proceeded to do our best. A mob of planters had by this time collected waiting to draw their coolie pay so back we all went to the Bank and paid out practically all the cash we had. There was no time to post any ledgers, all we could do was to pay out cash and hold the cheques in the till hoping to post them next day.

I phoned Kuala Lumpur and told Henderson the position and he said no more cash could be obtained but to ring again. I did on Sunday night and was told that he was sending down cars for me and to pack up and come away. I did not like doing it but with no staff and no cash it was impossible to carry on.

Two cars arrived and with my own in addition I was able to get away all the important books, small safe custody packets and all the cash except our copper supply which was too heavy and bulky to move. We actually left about 11pm on Sunday, the 4th January and as we could not have any lights on all the moving had to be done either in the dark or by torch light. The ledgers had been reposing in the back of my car each night for a week in case a quick getaway was called for. The Japs had attempted a landing from the sea north of Port Swettenham but had been driven off. Falconer, the District Officer, had all the European community up at his house that night with cars ready to make a getaway if necessary. I had the ledgers and the cash with me but after an anxious night we were able to go home again as the attack had been a failure. The remaining European women left for Singapore by car before midnight and got there safely. [We had already departed by sea].

I did not sleep above the Bank after that as the District Officer wanted us all to be close at hand in case any warnings came through. I slept in the ARP control room which had been moved to a house just below that of the DO but still had my meals in the flat. I may mention that I had an LDC (Local Defence Corps) guard in the Bank at night.

It had not been very pleasant living alone in the flat as I was practically the only person in the town at night except for ARP personnel on duty. An unearthly silence pervaded the place and the only sound was the drip of the rain coming through the roof at the other end of the flat. The servants did rig up a kind of Heath Robinson contraption of buckets and planks to try and catch the worst drips.

During the last couple of days or so I ran a branch of the Bank at the Club. This was to help planters who were in the Local Defence Forces and could not get off while the Bank was open. I used to take a few thousand dollars to the Club and cash cheques there for them. Very irregular banking, but it was greatly appreciated. [Father once mentioned how, before leaving Klang, they smashed all the bottles of whisky and spirits in the Club, this not just to spite the enemy but because of reported atrocities when Japanese soldiers had gained access to spirits. Father did comment that this task gave them a touch of schoolboy glee at the mischief done.]

I left Klang on the night of 4/5th January reaching Kuala Lumpur sometime after midnight. Henderson had an RAF lorry waiting so cash and books were at once transferred to it and sent off to Singapore.

It was now after 1am and the whole day had been just a bit too exciting. We had a few *stengahs* and badly needed they were, and so to bed. As events turned out I did not leave Klang any too soon as the Japs were there within a week.

A Note On The Bombing

Since coming to India I have often been asked what was the effect of a Jap bomb – but bombs were so erratic in their behaviour that it is difficult to predict what might happen.

For instance, in Klang a bomb was dropped on the pavement outside Dr Ansley Young's consulting room. The good doctor was under a table and unhurt and the building very slightly damaged whereas the Post Office which was on the other side of the road and set well back was badly knocked about, with numerous casualties. The doctor was a bit shaken, but was over at the Bank within five minutes to see if we were all right.

One of the most extraordinary incidents took place at the ARP Headquarters. They were protected by the usual wooden bunding but drains to carry away rain water from the roof passed under it at various places. A bomb burst about 10 yards outside and the blast passing through one of the drains blew Mrs Ormiston, our typist, right over the table at which she was sitting and she finished up on her hands and knees at the other side of the room about 12 feet away, shaken but unhurt. The blast from this same bomb severed the trunk of a large coconut palm about two feet from the ground as cleanly as if it had been done by a razor and lying on the ground beside this tree was Mr Goh Tiang Chin, a son of Mr Goh Hock Huat, a well-known constituent of the Bank. He was unhurt because he was lying down although only about six feet from the explosion. It cannot be too strongly emphasised that to lie down or get below the level of the ground means safety (short of a direct hit of course).

Another incident took place in the rest house compound, diagonally opposite the Bank. Trenches had been dug there and when the alarm went there were several people in the compound, Chinese and Indians. The Chinese got into the trench but the Indians stood under trees where they considered they could not be seen from above. They could not be persuaded to enter the trench. A bomb burst close by; the Chinese were unharmed but the two Indians were blown to pieces. It was most noticeable that even when a bomb burst on the hard surface of a road practically all the splinter marks on the surrounding walls were above the 18' level. Lie down and keep down. [Experience no doubt gained too as an Infantry Officer on the Western Front in World War One.]

Hamish: I've a few memories of the Klang raids. I saw and was shocked by how a piece of bomb had sliced right through one of the bunding's 6' square support beams and left the pale inner wood showing like some imagined wound. Father told me one story later how one of the staff was sheltering under the solid mahogany slab of counter during a raid when he felt something running down his neck. He began to think he was bleeding but all that had happened was a bottle of ink on the desk had been smashed by a bit of flying debris and the liquid had seeped down a joint in the counter to drop on to him.

We sheltered down in the bank's lower reaches, below ground level, and I can recall playing with the money, coins which were not to have much value shortly. Coins of the various denominations were wrapped in white paper, making small, solid cylinders (think Smarties tubes) which made fine building blocks for an eight year old who then of course 'bombed' them, our victorious RAF in action (at home anyway), my acting out what I was forever drawing.

As the most substantial building in Klang father thought it possible the Japanese would 'effect repairs and make use of the bank'. They did. In Compton Mackenzie's history of the Chartered (*Realms of Gold*) he records that Klang 'became the headquarters of the dreadful Japanese secret police, the Kempeitai, whose unfortunate victims were locked in the strong-rooms, and the sub-agent's own office was used as a torture chamber' – the room where we sheltered during raids.

One thing I recall clearly was the patriotic singing in the Singapore shelters! For years, later on, I'd be moved by hearing 'Land of Hope and Glory' sung, as at the last night of the Proms, for that was roared out then, as if to drown out the noise of the raids and declare defiance. My first musical memory! There was also the Vera Lynn song about the 'White Cliffs of Dover': 'There'll be blue birds over the White Cliffs of Dover/Tomorrow/Just you wait and see/There'll be love and laughter/And peace ever after/Tomorrow/When the world is free'. And we believed it.

When rubber went up it did so in churning pillars of black smoke, the last glimpse we had of Singapore as we departed on the *Marnix van St Aldegonde*.

Kuala Lumpur to Singapore

Having reached the Bank House in Kuala Lumpur in the early morning of 5th January 1941 I had a short spell during which I could take stock of things. Kuala Lumpur Office had received a direct hit from a bomb and the back part of the building was damaged so much that business had been transferred to the houses of the Accountant and Senior Sub-Accountant. The staff were carrying on under great difficulties, cramped for space, and inundated with demands for cash and for remittances out of the country. I assisted Mr Henderson to deal with the inward mails up at his house. The Post Office had been moved about two miles out of Kuala Lumpur and I went there in Henderson's car and collected the Registered Mails each day.

The first day I arrived just as the Jap planes came over so the sirens went and the Post Office closed down for the time being. The all clear went after about half an hour and I got the mail and returned with it to the Bank House. The second day the same thing happened except that the alert went when I was en route and I had to get out of the car and take cover in a large concrete drain. On each occasion the planes passed over Kuala Lumpur, evidently having business elsewhere.

The Bank house in Kuala Lumpur stands very high and one had a grand view of the Jap planes when they came over. There were a few anti-aircraft guns about, but they did not seem to cause the Japs any alarm for I never once saw one deviate from its allotted path because of them. One such gun was immediately behind the house and the first warning we usually got when planes appeared was the crash of it going off, a frightful noise at such close quarters and which made us dive for our dugout below the stairs *chop chop*.

The first day we had a visit from the Chief of Police in response to a phone message from the police in Klang. He asked me what I had done with the Sultan of Selangor's Regalia which was reposing in the strong room in Klang. I told him that it was still there and I was prepared to go back to Klang to get it out if necessary. However Henderson said that having got out of Klang safely I was on no account to go back but could hand over the keys to the police and let them deal with the matter. I carefully explained how to open the safe and I heard afterwards that, after a lot of trouble, they succeeded in doing so. They also removed, I was told, the valuables belonging to Japanese internees which had been deposited with us by the Military. The safe was then closed again and the keys I believe thrown into the Klang River. [London would later query why more had not been transported from Klang to Singapore. Father pointed out there was no transport or time, a polite 'Get real!']

The Government had promised Kuala Lumpur transport to move books and records to Singapore but when the time came all they sent was a small chemist's delivery van not capable of taking one tenth of what was required. Henderson's Air Force friends again came to the rescue and lent us a large six-ton truck. This was loaded up after dark on 6th January and sent off to Singapore. The European staff followed up next day in their own cars taking with them such of the local staff who volunteered to come.

I had filled up my tank on the afternoon of the 6th and also had a four gallon drum (a present from the RAF) on board. I had an RAF man with me and he was most useful for, being in uniform, we could obtain petrol at any of the military pumps en route. We filled up again at Gemas and kept our drum intact and it was fortunate we did so. About 30 miles from Johore Bahru I came on Peacock and Delacour both stopped for want of petrol. Being civilians they had been unable to obtain any from the military pumps and all others were closed down. I handed over my four gallon drum which enabled them to reach Singapore safely. We arrived at our temporary office in the Singapore Branch of the Yokohama Specie Bank just at dusk and so ended another stage of my journey.

The whole run had been without incident but the road cannot have been so quiet on other days judging by the number of wrecked cars lining the road, some evidently damaged by bombs and others with bullet holes through roof or windscreen. Jap planes were in the habit of patrolling the road and machine gunning but we saw nothing of them on the 7th January, just as well for the road was one long procession of cars. [This was the only day on which attacks were not continuously made on the road.]

One thing that struck me was the absence of the military. After Seremban I did not see a single camp and there were no obvious preparations being made to establish a line of defence across the peninsula at any point.

Hamish: 'Exit Klang' was published in June 1943 in the 'Chartered Bank Newsletter,' the Indian house organ of the bank (the regular London published magazine was called 'Curry and Rice'), edited by L J Blanchard, whom I recall as a family friend. Father would head for India after his escape and convalescence in South Africa for several more tumultuous years.

This newsletter also reported how a Mrs Moffat chose to get out of Jap-threatened Australia in February 1942. Off the American coast her ship was rammed by another accidentally and then, limping to port, was torpedoed and sunk. They were picked up by a destroyer which itself escaped the same fate, a torpedo seen passing within five feet of her.

There are two letters written just after the war which I find quite moving, and make me proud of father.

Chartered Bank, Klang. 19.10.45.
Dear Sir, I am pleased to hear from Mr R S B Unwin that you are safe in Madras and I take this opportunity to enquire after the health of Mrs Brown, young Hamish and your baby.

The Klang Branch is still unopen and I hope you will come back here to restart the business.

With best wishes, yours sincerely Lim Eng Jin. [Father replied on 12.11.45]

Chartered Bank, Klang. 30.11.45
My dear Sir, I thank you for your letter which I received last week and am very glad indeed to learn that you are safe and fit again, also that Mrs Brown, Hamish and the baby are all safe at home, therefore my dear Sir, let us all thank God Almighty for having been very kind to us during those dark days.

The first time I met Mr Henderson at Kuala Lumpur after the re-occupation by the British Forces, I enquired about you and Mr Miller (poor Mr Miller, it is very sad indeed to have lost him) but unfortunately, Mr Henderson was as much in the dark as I was concerning you both, and I would like to tell you how happy I feel when your letter came.

I did not reply to your letter earlier because the Chatwood Safe Company's experts came in here the day after your letter arrived and made arrangements to open the Strong Room door the following day and I thought that you might be interested to know the contents of the Strong Room. With the assistance of the Royal Engineers they managed to do so and I now enclose a list of the articles found therein. [a list of bank papers, most meaning little to the general public.]

There is practically nothing left of the Bank Property. Terrible looting was going on on the day the Japanese entered Klang. I came to town the very next day and had a look in at the office and what a sight. The floor was strewn with rubbish, torn books, papers and broken bits of furniture; the boxes belonging to Messrs D Reid and I C Mackay, kept near the press copy room, were broken and the contents missing. All the electric lamps were smashed, the railings over the counters had been pulled down; all that remained were those heavy furnitures and fittings that could not be moved. Upstairs it was no better. The piano, radios, refrigerators and everything removable were gone; even the Mount Fuji picture mentioned in your letters. Broken things and crockery were strewn all over the floor and some of the furniture was in bits – whatever things the looters could not remove, they destroyed. Oh Mr Brown, it was really a painful sight to see and to describe it further makes me sick.

A few days after occupation, the Japanese established their M A H Q at our premises. The counters were then intact. About a month later, several companies of their soldiers arrived. They then made the office their garrison and it continued to be so up to the time the British Forces took over. As soon as the Japs occupied the building, they took out all our old books, ledgers, files etc and made a bonfire of these just opposite the Bank where you will remember is a vacant plot of land by the side of the Oriental Bank of Malaya. They next removed the counters and I understand some portion they used as firewood. Many were the tales told of the happenings inside this garrison – of tortures, of deaths and other horrible things, but, thank God, everything is now over.

Some time last month, Messrs Kortright, Small and Hamilton visited Klang and it was then that Mr Kortright suggested that, as the business in Klang would be on a small scale, half of the building only would be sufficient while the other half, including the Junior Mess, could be rented out. His instructions are being carried out – one-half of the building is now partitioned off, new counters, furnitures and fittings made and fitted and we are trying our best to get the office going again, say by the middle of next month.

You will be glad to know that Captains Unwin and Rawcliffe are back again at Port Swettenham. Capt Rawcliffe told me that Capt Sheppard would join him some time next year. I D Macdonald was one of the first to arrive in Klang, then later came D Nicolson and M B Hember. With the exception of Mr Nicolson, all the rest of the above mentioned gentleman looked very well indeed, as a matter of fact, they have put on more weight since the last time I saw them in 1941.

Regarding Mr Goh Hock Huat, I am afraid the Japs had not been kind to him and he is now bedstricken. His son, Goh Tiang Chin, is quite well. Ah Tam is now running a small farm and is doing pretty well, even during the Japanese regime. As soon as I can, I shall pass on the good news to him. Your personal *tamby* [messenger], Shanmugam, was

121

very happy when I told him that you were safe and sound in Karachi and he asks me to convey to you his '*tabeks*' [greetings]. Eng Swee too is doing well.

Yes. With the exception of Toh Nee and a junior *tamby*, all the rest of the staff are OK. Everybody is eagerly looking forward to the day when we could start the office running again, the only regret is that we shall not have the pleasure of having you to open up the business and be with us again.

Life with me and my family was rather miserable. In the middle of 1942, I started out as a broker and managed to put through some deals in landed properties. These earnings together with the little savings I had, we managed to get along. In October '43, I lost my father. By March 1944, I found it unsafe to remain unemployed as there were then rumours of conscription; at the same time Japanese Gestapos and informers were very active. I immediately joined a Japanese firm, The Okuda Oil Mill Ltd (Boon Teck joining me). This concern took over Ng Tiong Kiat, Sin Teck Hong and Kuala Selangor Oil Mill factories (you remember these unfortunate companies I am sure) and was controlling the production of coconut oil. My salary was $190/- p.m. excluding bonus and allowances, but, owing to the very high cost of living this amount was insufficient, I had to turn to my saxophone for extra income. Playing at cafés, dinner parties, weddings and the like I averaged about $300/- a month and in this way (and with thanks to God's benevolence) managed to pull through.

Well Mr Brown, let me not bore you with more of this unpleasant topic; suffice it to say that I was lucky to get through. Now with reference to yourself, it is most regrettable that you are not due back in Klang soon. With your understanding and sympathy, you made it very pleasant working with you. I would therefore like to take this opportunity of thanking you for all the kindness you showed to me and my brother Boon Teck during your stay in Klang.

I am glad that you will be joining Mrs Brown and the children in Scotland soon and when you do, please give them my regards. Before closing, however, I would like to thank you once again and do sincerely hope that, after a well-earned rest, you will have the opportunity of coming back to Klang, a blessed day when you can be with us once again.

Yours sincerely Quay Hock Chuan.

PS Eng Jin wants me to inform you that he received your letter a few days back and will be replying soon.

The spread of Japan's attacks was unforeseen – and hard to believe – Pearl Harbor, then China's Treaty Ports, the Philippines, Malaya, Hong Kong (fell on Christmas Day 1941) Singapore (February 15), Sumatra soon after, Java by the end of February, Burma at the same time. So many fronts. So few defences.

Father's bank, the Standard Bank of India, Australia and China, saw its eastern establishments swept away in just a few months, in reality its world reduced to just India and Ceylon. (It never operated in Australia.) Over a hundred European staff were captured, seventeen lost their lives. Many were to be saved by an exchange of civilian captives arranged at Lourenco Marques in late August 1942 but for the rest there was a further three years of desperate privation. Those interned in Singapore were treated with great cruelty and several with any military connections from Malaya ended working on the Burma railway with all that entailed. Father was so lucky to escape.

In the period before the Japanese arrived the bank faced endless problems. In Malaya life operated very much on a credit system with goods signed for, or services at clubs and hotels employing 'chits,' with settlement made monthly. As soon as the Japanese invasion started all that ended. Salaries began to be paid weekly. Father was trying to pay out monies right until the end, when there was no more money. Once Japanese had control of the country they then introduced their own money.

Singapore and Afterwards

As previously reported I travelled by car from Kuala Lumpur to Singapore on 7th January. I went first to the office in Meyer Chambers where the books etc. were unloaded and placed in as safe a place as possible as the strong room was not available. Accommodation had been arranged for us by Singapore Office and Peacock, Delacour and I were put up at the Adelphi Hotel, where conditions appeared to be normal.

Meyer Chambers was already occupied by the branches which had reached Singapore before us and by Guthrie & Co. and there was no room for us. Guthrie & Co. whose own premises, next our Singapore Office, had been bombed and completely destroyed had arranged to vacate Meyer Chambers at the end of the week and it was therefore decided that Kuala Lumpur and Klang should delay opening to the public until the Monday after our arrival.

The interval was fully occupied in complying with the various Government regulations as to registration and preparing books and stationery ready for opening. Conditions in Singapore seemed to be normal and it was hard to believe that fighting was taking place at the time just north of Kuala Lumpur.

None of the Klang staff had come to Singapore and it was impossible to obtain any assistance from the other

Branches who were all very short staffed. I engaged one man locally who had been with the KPM and had had ledger experience but his lack of knowledge of banking routine was a big handicap and meant that I had to write all slips myself and scrutinise every entry very carefully.

We opened for business on the Monday and were inundated with requests for drafts and TT remittances. The actual issue of the drafts and despatch of the telegrams was done by Kuala Lumpur as being alone it was quite impossible for me to do so but I passed the slips and entries and was responsible that all remittances were paid for before despatch. I may here mention that there were many expressions of gratitude from our upcountry clients when they found that our ledgers were in Singapore and that their accounts could be operated on normally. It must be remembered that most of them had lost everything and that a small credit balance represented all they possessed in the world. The wives of most of our upcountry clients were already in Singapore and the men themselves were gradually coming in as the fighting line approached the Island. We were kept extremely busy and although we closed to the public at noon we were never out of the office before dark although towards the end we had to get home earlier to be off the streets before the curfew and the total blackout commenced.

Air raid alerts were a daily occurrence but to begin with were confined to the night. Latterly however when the Japs approached Singapore and it was possible for them to give their bombers fighter protection day raids became more frequent and during the last week air raids were more or less continuous. Business under these conditions became more and more difficult. We carried on under these difficult conditions until Thursday, the 12th February, when the Government intimated that they could not supply us with any more currency. This of course meant the virtual closing down of the Banks and business came to a standstill.

Friday 13th morning (Black Friday) was spent destroying codes and various documents but no business was done with the public. Peacock and I went back to the Adelphi for *tiffin* and although all the native staff had fled we were able to get a satisfactory meal by helping ourselves in the kitchen. Just as we were leaving shelling started and part of the roof of the Roof Garden was blown off. Shelling continued on our way back to the office and we had to take shelter in the Town Hall for about an hour. We eventually reached our Singapore office where we took shelter in the *tiffin* room which had been set up in the basement. While there, Columbine, the Singapore Accountant, came and told me that there was a ship going that afternoon and that those who were prepared to take the risk were free to go.

Kyle and Beath set off for the wharf and I followed them to find out from which jetty the ship was leaving. I then went back to Meyer Chambers and passed the word round that there was an opportunity to get out. I had a suit case prepared for such an eventuality and I opened it and having abstracted the pages containing the latest current account balances and also rough Cash Book entries from the date on which the balances were taken I packed them in my case together with up to date records of fixed deposits and fixed loans.

I then went down to the wharf and found that only those with passes were being permitted through the gate. No mention had been made of passes and no one in Meyer Chambers had been given the opportunity to obtain one. I cannot speak for Singapore Office but I believe that they were in the same position as we were. While I was at the gate D M Millar of Singapore appeared and as he had a pass he was allowed through. He endeavoured to get me through on his pass but this was not allowed. Shortly after D W Henderson of Kuala Lumpur appeared also with a pass and he said he would arrange for my pass after he was through. Whether he did or not I do not know for shortly after I saw a friend who was with the PWD in Klang on the right side of the gate and as he was able to vouch for me I was allowed through.

I then went forward to the wharf where the tender which was to take us to our ship was lying and it was while there that the wharf was bombed, the nearest bomb being about 50 yards away. There were a number of casualties as there was no shelter but I was untouched. This bombing was most unfortunate as it meant that a considerable number of wounded were brought on our ship which had no proper accommodation for them. I went on board the tender and shortly after it left for the ship which was at anchor about half a mile out. Another raid then took place and bombs were again dropped on the wharf and godowns and also in the sea between the shore and our ship. Two, I think, people on our ship were killed by splinters and a few others injured. It was now about dusk and after another tender had discharged its cargo of passengers we set sail. There must have been about five to six hundred people on board but no roll call was taken so no one knew who was on board. There were however no other Chartered Bank men on this ship, the *Kuala* (954 tons).

Shortly after leaving we passed Puloh Bukum where the large APC refinery is situated. This had been on fire for days and was still a mass of flame and smoke when we passed. Puloh Samboe was passed about midnight and the Dutch refinery there was just a sea of flame with the palms on the beach silhouetted against the blaze. We were very cramped for space on the boat and sleep was next to impossible.

127

The Kuala, *father's ill fated ship (drawing)*

We anchored in the lee of a small Dutch island, Pom Pong, (next to Benku Island), at daybreak on the 14th February as it was not considered safe to sail during the day and were shortly after joined by another ship, the *Tien Kwong* which had been accompanying us. We tied up about half a mile from the shore and about two miles off there was a third ship which had been bombed the day before but not sunk. She was anchored and had been abandoned. [She was the *Kung Wo* and had left Singapore the day before with another ship, the *Shu Kwang*, the latter having been sunk.]

After breakfast which consisted of a division of the few tins of food available it was decided to camouflage the ship as a precaution against possible air attack and I was one of a party of about 30 that went ashore in the ships' boats to cut branches to do this. I never gave aeroplanes a thought as we were about one hundred miles south of Singapore and thought that all Jap planes would be too busy there to worry about small ships like ours [800 tons].

However, while ashore, a reconnaissance plane came over to be followed shortly after by 7 Jap bombers. They evidently came over to finish off the ship which they had bombed the day before and not sunk, for they attacked her and she was hit and under the water in about five minutes. They next came for us and got a direct hit just forward of the bridge at their first attempt. The bomb landed just where the sick bay had been established and all those wounded on the wharf on the previous day must have been wiped out. The ship was now on fire and the fire was soon out of control as the steam pipes had been broken by the explosion and it was impossible to use the fire fighting equipment.

People were by this time jumping into the sea and making for the island but a considerable number must have been carried away by the very strong tide. The two boats which had been ashore were both doing excellent work picking up survivors but they could not hope to cope with such a large number. The numbers were increased by the passengers and crew from the *Tien Kwong* although it had not been hit. They all jumped overboard and made for the shore and there must have been close on one thousand people in the water at one time. The Jap planes circled round and coming back dropped bombs among the swimmers then back again some ten minutes later and bombed the beach where a considerable number of people had landed. A lot of people lost their lives here as the shore was precipitous and part of the cliff was blown down on top of them.

Whether or not this bombing of survivors was deliberate

I cannot say as the planes were at a considerable height and it may have been an attempt to bomb the *Tien Kwong*. I was on shore all this time and although I did not see the bombs actually hitting the ship I saw all that happened afterwards, a dreadful sight, the ship in flames and the people jumping into the sea and being carried away by the tide. All my belongings were of course in the ship, including the Bank records, and were all lost. I was left with nothing except what I stood up in, shorts, shoes, stockings and I was better off than most in having shoes and stockings as these were discarded by those who had to swim. [*Singapore to Freedom* (see Notes) gives many more details, the writer, Gilmour, was aboard when the *Kuala* was hit. He also notes that two other ships, the *Dragonfly* and the *Grasshopper* had left Singapore only to be attacked. The former sank almost at once but the *Grasshopper* was able to run aground on another island in the Rhiow archipelago.]

Survivors were scattered all along the beach but gradually collected into two large parties, one opposite the ship and the other consisting of those who had been carried to the other end of the Island by the current. In this second party were most of those from the *Tien Kwong* which was still afloat but who had made for the shore when the bombing started.

The Jap planes came back again in the afternoon and dropped bombs including some delayed action, indiscriminately over the island without causing any damage or casualties. We were very fortunate in finding a spring of fresh water near the place where we originally landed to cut camouflage and where the first party camped. The second party on the other side of the island were not so fortunate and could not find water and were eventually forced to join up with the first party. We got a certain quantity of supplies from the *Tien Kwong* but these did not amount to a great deal when the number of about seven hundred on the island was taken into consideration. A considerable number of causalities were landed and the lack of medical supplies was acutely felt. Our first day's ration consisted of one ounce of Bully Beef and half a biscuit plus half a cigarette tin of water. We were afraid to be more liberal until we knew exactly how we were placed.

The island was uninhabited but the supply position tended to improve as people left us and natives from neighbouring islands brought provisions. The other Bank men now on the island were, D M Millar, D W Henderson, Purser and Hamilton, all of whom had been on the *Tien Kwong*. (It was feared that Henderson was lost as he did not appear until two days after the landing but he eventually turned up rather the worse for wear. The others were fit with the exception of Millar who had a small injury to his forehead.)

To simplify the distribution of water and rations we organised into parties of twelve presumably because there are 12 ozs. of Bully Beef in the tin and 1 oz was our ration. The spring which supplied us with water was put out of bounds to all but a party of six who were responsible for the drawing of water and its dispatch to the distributing point which was established about 50 yards away. This was most important so as to prevent pollution of our only supply of water and worked well. I was one of the party at the spring and although monotonous it gave me something to do and prevented the ennui which most seemed to suffer. It was most noticeable that those who had work to do were much more contented than those who were only too pleased to lie about and do nothing.

Rations continued to be small but it was really wonderful how one got used to living on next to nothing provided that water was available and in this direction the fates were

131

kind. At its peak we drew about 170 gallons a day from our spring but towards the end of our stay there was a distinct falling off in the flow and a few more days on the island might have made conditions serious. Rain might have fallen of course but we all considered that we were fortunate in having a spell of very unusual dry weather while on our island. Rain would have been a tragedy for the injured in the absence of any shelter.

The first lot to leave us were about two hundred women and children and wounded taken off on Monday night on the *Tanjong Pinang* and not heard of since. [Father added 'Since the above was written the *Times*, London, has published the information that *Tanjong Pinang* had been captured and sunk by the Japanese and all on board taken prisoner'.] On Wednesday, the 18th February, a Japanese-motor fishing boat in charge of an ex tin-miner, named Reynolds, appeared and took off about one hundred including most of the remaining wounded. [There were now 200 women and children, 30-40 civilian men and 400 military on the island.]

On Friday, the 20th, three Chinese Junks appeared along with the motor boat and everyone, Millar, Purser, Hamilton and I were in the motor boat, D W Henderson elected to come in one of the Junks. I did not see him again but trust that he got away. [Henderson did not get away and was last seen in Padang (since reported a prisoner)]. The motor boat left just at dusk and headed for the mouth of the Indragiri River which was reached about midnight. We tied up until 3am during which time the Captain had a sleep. He gave the course to the helmsman and went back to sleep but it appears that the helmsman took the instructions to be South East when they should have been South West so for three hours we sailed in the wrong direction. When the Captain discovered the mistake we must have been well away from the coast again so we had to retrace our route. We lost six hours over this mistake and they were not pleasant as Jap planes passed over frequently but they had business elsewhere or considered our boat too small to bother about. We eventually reached Prigi Radjah at the mouth of the Indragiri River about mid-day.

We stopped there but were instructed to proceed up river to Tembilihan which we reached about 4.30pm. The trip up the river was uneventful and no more Jap planes were seen. Tembilihan was a small native village more or less deserted but in peacetime it must have done a thriving trade in copra as there were quantities lying about. The few shops that were open were invaded but there was very little to be had, my purchases consisted of a toothbrush, an enamel spoon and a sarong, the last to give me a chance to wash the very grubby shirt and shorts which were all I possessed and which were much the worse for wear. A good wash down in cold water was most welcome but there was still no possibility of a shave for any of us.

At dusk we were all taken to a school and given a meal of rice and boiled duck eggs and after a week's starvation didn't it taste good to feel something inside again. We slept the night on the floor of a copra godown, our first night under cover since leaving Singapore. Next day we had more rice and eggs and were also able to buy the finest pineapples I have ever tasted. At mid-day we left again by river, our motor boat in charge of Reynolds towing another ship about twice its size whose engines had broken down.

I was unfortunate in being assigned to the towed ship which although larger had much less deck space and that available being steel and very dirty. Five of us selected a wooden bench thinking we were lucky but at the end of our 23 hours sail we were not quite so certain about our luck.

Anyone who has attempted to sit on a narrow wooden bench for 23 hours will appreciate how we felt (or rather the absence of feeling by that time.) It was bitterly cold during the night and it was impossible to move to try and get warm; in fact, this was the most uncomfortable part of the whole journey.

We reached Ringat at about 9.30am on the morning of 23rd February and found that most of the population were still there. It was a bigger place than Tembilihan and we were able to change our Straits dollars into local money and make some small purchases. I had my first shave since leaving Singapore and a layer of at least an inch had to be removed. Five razors were used, each one blunter than its predecessor, a painful ordeal, but the end justified the means. I also got sundry rents in my shorts repaired and not having any spares in my wardrobe had to stand in my equally torn shirt while the repairs were effected much to the interest of a crowd of natives who collected round the shop door. Back to the godown opposite our landing place where we had a meal, our first fresh vegetables, and then on by bus to a large Rubber Factory (Ayer Molok Estate) about 30 miles away.

Things here were very well organised and we were made up into parties of about twelve, each party being numbered, my number was 46, the numbering to facilitate our departure by bus or lorry to the other side of Sumatra. Work in the factory had closed down and we were billeted in a large new packing shed with crêpe rubber sheets for bedding. There was unlimited fresh water here and the coagulating tanks made ideal baths. We had our first real bath, washed all our filthy clothing and for the first time since leaving Singapore felt clean again. We had a really good rest – and were ready for it. We did nothing but eat and sleep during the two days at Ayer Molok. W M Ritchie and D Lowdon were in camp when we arrived having got there two days before us. As far as they knew no others had been able to get away from Singapore. [This escape route operated till transport ran out. Unfortunately the Japs were to capture 700 who were stranded there.]

We left Ayer Molok by bus at mid-day on 25th February for Sawah Loentoh at the rail head on the other side of Sumatra. The road was very rough and the going very bumpy at times but it was interesting seeing a part of the world which none of us would otherwise have seen. The road ran parallel with the Indragiri River for a time and on this stage there was a considerable amount of cultivation. Afterwards we started to climb and passed through very wild country. The road at no time reached more than three to four thousand feet but the whole country seemed to be a wilderness of never-ending hills. We were still in the hills when darkness fell and the remaining time until we arrived at 11.30 appeared to be all through hilly country. We had a good deal of rain as well which made the very erratic driving even more hair-raising but we got through with only a broken fan belt.

On arrival at Sawah Loentoh we found the hotel where we were to be accommodated full up. Seven elected to stay there and sleep on the floor but five chose to go on to other accommodation which was available at a mining school about a mile out of the town. I went on and we were most comfortable in a small cubicle which in other times had been used by the students at the mining school. Each cubicle had two beds and it was very pleasant to be in a bed again and have a good night's rest.

Sawah Loentoh is a prosperous little mining town and is joined to Padang by rail. Coal has been mined there for many years and work was still under way while we were there. The place had an air of prosperity and business appeared to be going on as usual.

We left Sawah Loentoh by train at 4.30am on 27th February and reached Padang about noon. This was a most interesting part of our journey. The country was all cultivated and we passed through a seemingly endless procession of terraced paddy fields. They stretched for mile after mile and the amount of work involved in making all the terraces must have been immense. The native villages were all very neat and tidy and much cleaner than the equivalent in Malaya. We were told that villages were fined if cleanliness was not up to standard and that the peasants were fined if their land was not properly cultivated. (Judging by results this is a system which might well be copied by any future administration in Malaya.) Food on this part of the journey was very plentiful and we lived royally on rice, corn cobs, banana fritters, oranges and other local produce. We were interested to see this as at the back of our minds was the thought that we might not be able to get away from Sumatra but have to take to the hills and live on the country for the duration. Incidentally this was the cheapest railway journey I had ever done, seven hours in the train for 92 Dutch cents.

On arrival at Padang we were most hospitably received by the residents. We were fitted out with a few spare clothes, but there was not much choice owing to the large numbers that had arrived before us. I got a coat which fitted fairly well but the only trousers available were about six inches too long and a foot too large in circumference. However, scissors and a belt saved my reputation. I was billeted with a Dutch lady and was very well looked after. She did the necessary repairs to my limited wardrobe and also washed the things I had arrived in. I am most grateful to her.

We were two days in Padang and it was nice to be able to visit shops and supplement our meagre belongings. We were visited by Jap planes daily but no bombs were dropped in the town although the docks which are about five miles away appeared to get some attention. There must have been about two thousand of us in Padang and we were all very worried as the Japs were gradually approaching and there was no defence whatever in Padang. A few parachute troops could have taken the place with ease and why they did not was a mystery as Padang was the only port left in Sumatra.

Our headquarters had been established in a very nice club (Eendracht Club) and we kept in touch in case any news came through. I called there on Sunday afternoon about 4.30 and was told to catch a train at 5 as ships were expected, and to get down to the harbour immediately. It did not take me long to pack my few belongings in a blue handkerchief, say goodbye to my hostess, and get along to the station. On arrival at the harbour it was a wonderful sight to see a British destroyer alongside. As many as she could carry were packed in and at dusk off we went out to sea at full speed. One of the crew of this destroyer was J D Moss, an ex-planter from the Klang district. We went full speed for about 30 miles and were then transferred to a cruiser, HMAS *Hobart*, the destroyer returning for more. As soon as we were on board the cruiser set off at full speed to be out of bombing range before dawn and then settled down to a steady cruising pace until we reached the south coast of Ceylon on the afternoon of 5th March. Our trip on the cruiser was most enjoyable as it was the first time any of us had felt safe since leaving Singapore on 13th February. [There was still the threat of submarines.] There must have been about 700 of us and most had to sleep on deck but this was no hardship after what we had come through. One of the officers kindly offered me the use of his cabin and I felt I was in the lap of luxury.

137

I had already been stationed in Colombo and it was like coming home to be entering the well-known harbour again. Arrangements for our reception were excellent and no praise can be too high for the efforts made to look after us by the Colombo residents. All were given billets and were most hospitably received. Millar, Lowden, Ritchie, Purser and I were kindly put up by Mr Wemyss and Hamilton by Mr Hendrie. The food situation in Ceylon, however, was not too good and they were very anxious that we should all leave again as soon as possible. We spent our time there supplementing our depleted wardrobes. Eventually we were put on board a ship on which we remained for four days in the harbour under very bad conditions. The Naval and Military personnel were given first and second class accommodation, civilians being put below decks in quarters resembling the Black Hole of Calcutta. Tepid water and a small ration of lukewarm watery beer were the only drinks at one time as even the second class saloon was put out of bounds and we were not to encroach on that part of the deck allotted to our Naval and Military friends. Feeling ran very high as the same members of the forces had been given the free run of our houses and clubs in Malaya over many months, and they made no effort to reciprocate. Our position was so impossible that a deputation was sent ashore to interview the Evacuation Committee. They were most indignant at our treatment having been given to understand that, although there would be a shortage of sleeping accommodation, we would be free to make use of all the amenities of the ship. They arranged for our transfer to another ship with much better accommodation. We were very grateful. We eventually left for Durban on the 19th March, 1942, arriving on the 27th after an uneventful voyage, on the *Nieuw Amsterdam*.

Since coming to Durban, I have been asked many times why a place like Singapore did not put up a better show. In the first place was Singapore the impregnable fortress it was supposed to be? Defences on the land side seemed to be entirely lacking or were most inefficient. Why, when it became apparent that the Japs were coming down the peninsula, was no effort made to construct lines of defence right across at various strategic positions. The absence of any prepared positions was most noticeable on the way down from Klang to Singapore. Why was a Siamese delegation allowed to inspect the defences of Singapore a few weeks before the showdown? Our intelligence seems to have been entirely misled. Why such a lack of air power? Our fighters, Brewster Buffalos, were about 40 miles per hour slower than the Jap bombers and it was rather pathetic and tragic to see how easily they could get away or circle round and come up behind their pursuers. The anti-aircraft defences in Singapore were very good and Jap bombers were always kept at a good height, but in Klang there was no defence and the Japs could come down over the roof tops with impunity. Why were reinforcements being landed when it must have been obvious Singapore was doomed? Troops were actually being evacuated by the ships which brought reinforcements. There are so many whys that it is impossible to recapitulate them all but in my opinion a dominant factor was the lack of resolute leadership in a position of danger. It was a sorry business and there will be a lot of dirty linen to be washed in public at the close of the war.[6]

In conclusion, I would like to put in a word for the very good work done by the civilian population of Singapore, especially the Eurasian and Chinese shopgirls and telephone operators. That business was able to carry on until two days before the capitulation was in no small measure due to them and my personal feelings are that I am proud

139

to have been a civilian in Singapore at a very difficult time in its history.

Hamish: Father's initial account of his experiences after we left him at Klang was written in pencil, 55 pages of it, in his illegible banker's handwriting, in a reporter's notebook. I only undertook the daunting task of transcribing it many years after his death and the note book is now in the National Library of Scotland collections. Only now have I come on his own typed copy, which is signed and dated 10.9.42. It was sent to the Chartered in London, who were 'most interested indeed' to receive it. A reply, dated 20.11.42, was sent to Bombay where father was sailing 'for orders'. 'We are very pleased to learn you have made such a good recovery ... and I trust you will have no return of your trouble in India'. Sadly, 'not a single word has emanated from either Malaya or the Dutch East Indies since they fell into the hands of the Japanese, and I fear all who were in Singapore when the city capitulated are now in internment. It is all terribly tragic ... '

The letter was a curiosity in itself as the letter was typed on a prepared form which was then photographically reduced to a 5' x 4' size for transmission, a wartime effort to save bulk and weight for overseas mail. Father regularly commented on the bank's consideration of its staff and their loyalty and friendliness to each other. Life was not just all *tiffin* and tennis. I find it admirable that father still had a suitcase of bank papers and records when he managed to join the ill-fated *Kuala*, a duty he would have taken for granted.

Perhaps the Japanese scorn for the surrender had some justification. They – the Japanese – were very nearly out of ammunition and food supplies and could probably have been checked by vigorous action. The British and Australian

140

forces on the other hand were mostly raw newcomers who had never been trained in jungle fighting, our air defences had been destroyed, and there was no naval presence. Nevertheless almost anything would have been better than surrendering 130,000 troops, and a million civilians (today's population is over three million) and handing the enemy a massive arsenal of guns and ammunition – 55,000 rifles (with 18 million rounds of ammunition) and 2,300 machine guns for a start.

The highly successful Japanese General in Malaya, Yamashita, was seen as a possible new political force in Tokyo so Hideki Tojo's reward for his success was a posting to Manchuko (Manchuria) – the equivalent of a Stalin posting to Siberia.

The Japanese advance was shockingly fast. The Japanese landed on 7 December 1941 in Siam and the extreme north of Malaya and K.L. fell on 11 January and Singapore surrendered on 15 February. It was assumed the jungle terrain would be difficult but the Japanese (with tanks) simply advanced rapidly down the main road and, if held up at all, merged into the jungle to outflank such defences. The infantry used thousands of bicycles. So fast was the advance that very seldom were the Allies even able to blow up vital bridges in their retreating. The Japanese also made frequent landings by sea to bypass defences. It was a *blitzkrieg* which our forces could neither withstand, nor understand. Japan was considered a militarily backward force while we still had our remnant of inbred superiority. But Japan's proclaimed ambition of creating a Greater East Asia, free of foreigners, would prove a myth. They treated most 'liberated' countries with brutal insensitivity, massacring tens of thousands of Chinese in Malaya for instance. Instead of being liberators they were the worst of conquerors. Japan was not to bring independence; that

141

the various people would do themselves, in their own time. With Australia threatened, the Japanese impetus slowed and stopped (the Battle of Midway in early June saw four of their six great carriers sunk). Lines of supply had become over extended and thereafter it was Japan, often fighting with a ferocious disregard for life, which was in long retreat till the end: the horrors of Hiroshima on 6 August 1945 and Nagasaki three days later. Emperor Hirohito ordered Japan's surrender on 14 August: VJ Day.

One who watched the Japanese surrender on board the US battleship *Missouri* in Tokyo Bay was Singapore's General Percival. He and other VIPs had been imprisoned in Manchuria. Tojo tried to commit suicide but was duly hanged. Yamashita fought on in the Philippines after the surrender but would suffer the same fate.

This is all a long time ago now and if one picks up any book on Japan or Malaysia or Singapore today the war is just one episode, covering only a few years, and not really meaning very much today, to a population born since the war and whose lives have been filled with other sorrows, other joys. No one in the days described could imagine what these countries would look like in their grandchildren's eyes, no more than the grandchildren can imagine the colonial past of their grandparents. Perhaps the best place to be living is the present. Not that we should forget while grandparents still remember. Our today springs from what they did, and who they were, then.

Sitting on my desk is a very personal reminder of those days. I see it every day, often many times every day; a shattered piece of Yale-style lock, smashed by a flying piece of bomb as father reached for the handle. The door was to the family flat above the bank, the flat roof a good observation post for fire-watching, part of father's ARP duties. I sometimes use the heavy bit of lock to hold open a book, more than once I have given myself a wee cut on its jagged edges, but it remains on my desk, both a *memento mori*, and a testimony to life.

8

South Africa

Mother must have felt a tremendous relief on reaching Durban safely with her two charges, David, 13 months, and Hamish, 8, but she must have had the deepest fears about what might be happening to her Billie. Just one South African letter survives but her 1941 pocket diary continued on from the last page with brief entries: 'Jan 1, 1942. Sailing, Batavia [Java; soon to be over-run by the Japanese and the capital renamed Jakarta.] 19: Durban. 20: Bank. Cables. Woolworths. Toys. Pram.'

The bank would have no news and a cable to Singapore was returned, the one home is referred to in a letter of Ian's. The name Edith and Nellie often appear: they were sister-in-law and sister of father's, Jim and Edith being resident in South Africa and Nellie with husband, a military doctor, there coping with evacuees as we refugees were called. Mother never stopped referring to our luck in having family in South Africa. There was so much practical as well as business matters to cope with. We spent much time on the vast Durban beach, cousin Dickie often with us. The stress shows. 'Jan 31: Edith's. Dream – parachutists. Tipplar, Schooler, who got out; Feb 1: Ham bed fever [Days were spent at Kloof, Botha's Hill, and Hill Crest looking for somewhere to stay and where I could go to

Safe! Dickie, Mother, David and Hamish on the beach at Durban, 1942.

yet another school. Botha's Hill was named after an early settler, Philip Rudolph; a grandson was Louis, general in the Boer War and first Prime Minister of South Africa]; 10 Feb: Women's Auxiliary morning [a regular Tuesday date while in Durban]; 15 Feb: fall of Singapore. Bad sleep. Cardew here. Tawney [others who had escaped]; 23 Feb: Walk H Durban School; 26 Feb: Budge telephoned; 27 Feb: Budge Durban [and other escapee names appearing]; 4 Mar: Sumatra news; 6 Mar: Cable from B, Colombo: 'Lost everything but safe love Brown'; 10 Mar: Cable B; 23 Mar: B's cable 'coming'. 27 Mar B arrived.'

Father had earlier been ill in Japan and, whatever it was this time, he needed a year of sick leave in South Africa to recover from 'such a bad time' as a friend called it. There are frequent notes of 'B Durban. Doctor'. The wee diary entries ended in early May. There was still the problem of being reunited with Ian and Gran, either in South Africa or Scotland but neither was practical for non-combatants with the risk of submarine attacks at sea. There are letters of twelve year old Ian to South Africa which give hints of the home concern.

Ian and Gran stayed with Aunt Iza in Dunfermline to see in the New Year. Some of them went to a Polish concert. Ian: 'Three engine-room artificers were in and we had a good time. One of the naval men showed me how to stick a silver-paper-egg-cup to the ceiling. I was up till two o'clock but then we slept till 11am'. Aunt Iza regularly had Polish officers staying in her house. When she died a shelf of Polish books came my way. I was staying with Aunt Iza when VJ day was declared with all the razzmatazz that produced. Strangely, in Ian's letters there is no reference to the war in Europe at all. 'Jan 7: Gran and I are both very glad to hear you are on your way to Durban. All that was in the cable was, "write c/o Jim, Effie Brown" ... The new

146

teacher Miss Macquarie arrived on the *Comet* ... Jan 11:
I am glad Hamish's books arrived. I sent them off in June.
Your pullover and sweets arrived. You are a very good
knitter. Everyone is asking us about you and daddy. Gran
and I would love to be out with you in Durban but we will
have to wait and hear what Daddy says. I hope Hamish
and David were not too much trouble on board. Gran will
cable Daddy when things are more settled... Feb 7: I hope
you and the brothers are well and you have settled down
nicely with Uncle Jim. Gran says Durban is a fine place
with a good beach so Hamish will love swimming. I hope
you have had good news from Daddy. Feb 14: I got two of
your letters which were posted on 11 and 27 November.
Guessing David's weight sounded an interesting way to
raise money.

Feb 23: I would like to write to Daddy but we do not
know where he is but will post them when the Head Office
tells us. Ever so many people have been asking after you all.
I hope you have heard about Daddy before now. Hamish
will cheer you up I am sure with saying daft things. Aunt
Dor is very kind to us in Rosemount and I like Carrick.
Mar 8: I am very glad Daddy is in Sumatra. I hope he
will soon be in Ceylon. Oh, we are glad you are all safe.
We are in deep snow at Southpark in Cove. I came on the
Comet from Carrick and walked from the pier at Kilcreg-
gan to give Gran a surprise, walking in on her. Mar 14:
South Park, Cove. Dear Daddy, we are very very pleased
to hear that you are safe in Colombo. The cable came this
morning. Your birthday. Gran met me at the pier with the
good news. Hope you have some friends and celebrate. My
birthday is on Monday. I brought a tin of chocolates from
Carrick which you kindly sent from Klang. We do knitting
at school and, of course, in any spare time .... We received
a letter from you written on the 1st December...'

147

Gran was house-minding for friends and Ian travelled to Cove for weekends. The *Comet* was still operating at the end of the war when we had family holidays in Carrick but soon after was sold and last heard of on the Congo. To reach Carrick today one has to make a limited, tedious bus run via Loch Lomond and the Rest and Be Thankful.

'Ap 3: Is Hamish at a big school? You sound happy in South Africa. I think Carrick School will fizzle out. Andy leaves in summer, I go to Dollar and two others may not return so it won't be kept for one pupil. Apr 26: We've just received a letter written by Daddy from Singapore ... I hope Daddy is with you by now at Hillcrest which is a very nice name ... May 28: Yesterday Aunt Dorothy got four tons of coal which was dumped at the gate as the lorry couldn't get through. She did not know it was coming. It took me three hours to get it in. We've been catching eels for a friend's kitten to eat. June 14: We went up to Corriemonachan, Aunt Dor taking the boat for wood. The woodman had cut it and we carried it down to the rocks. We had tea and a bathe and went out fishing. We then loaded the boat and walked home. You say Cousin Bunny is going to be in the SAAF. Is he to be a pilot or a gunner? Does Hamish have a sense of humour for he reports, "In the sack race I was second – and last"?' [This was at Highbury School. In mother's phrase I obviously still had the habit of 'coming out with things'. At the dinner table I informed a visitor who had left some food, 'In this house we always clean our plates'.]

Bunny was Uncle Jim's older boy, Dickie, my companion the other. Sadly, Bunny in the South African Air Force, was to disappear over Germany later in the year. In August on a visit to Dollar, Gran and Ian visited the Patons (grandparents of my friend in Klang) and were told Mr Paton and his two brothers were still missing. Ian was in Dollar being kitted out for starting school there after the holidays. They managed to find accommodation above the fish shop at 11 Station Road – where we would join them in late 1944. Douce Ian must have received a considerable shock with two lively brothers suddenly appearing. I spoke with a strong South African twang.

Hamish in Highbury school uniform, South Africa, 1942.

The one letter of mother's is intriguing in that it includes news of her mother, Gran, having a romance. This is the first (and last) I'd ever known of it.

Botha's Hill Hotel. 31 July 1942.
To Gran, from Mummy. Beginning your scrawl and having just written you an air-graph letter makes me long to fly home to you. Capt S sounds nice and don't you hesitate and waste time if you feel like it. Ian could easily stay with you or board. It's your own affair entirely but please don't let Ian or any of us stand in your way. Don't dare to think for a minute that you are a nuisance, you have done a real war job looking after Ian so well, look how much happier he is than if boarding. If he hadn't been with you, I would have had to risk the two young ones on the sea long before this. Priceless, you and your boyfriend, it's been fun and I wonder if it will be more!

Lot more sensible than Mrs R's bloke. He sounds like a lot of evacuees in this country who get us all such a bad name, won't stop grumbling and seem to forget there is a war on and won't even attempt to adapt to a different way of living. Jolly comfy in this hotel, splendid Indian waiters. Dickie has just gone and very sorry to go. He got a lift by car from Freeman, the hotel owner, much better than train, especially as we are having our first rain for a couple of weeks. Ham and David playing so nicely on the veranda, the big dog always with them. He had some grand walks with Dickie this last week, off on their hunting expeditions. Lucky with weather for Ham's holidays, both in Durban and here, cold, dry and sunny. Wonder if you went to Tiree. [They did, staying at Salum Guest House, Ruaig, and Tiree would see our first holiday when all united again.]

Dollar seems all right during school terms and you seem to like it and have plenty friends. I'm glad you have Mrs

150

Paton, such a nice comfy person, generous like Dorothy but not so queer tempered. Bet you have far more friends in Dollar alone than Iza has in all Dunfermline with all her life spent there. Here Nellie seems lonely (recently widowed) and loves having us in spite of the squash it makes in her tiny flat. I've got a watch for Ian, a real good one, water-proof, shock-proof and heaven knows what else. Mary Cardew will take it. She hopes to leave soon on the ship where her brother is doctor, a great help as her three weans are terrors (boys older and younger than Ham and little girl like David). They have had bad luck with lots of illness. She is such a pet, very good looking, young and tall, one of the very nicest women I've ever met but rather helpless. Her husband is twenty years older and a regular army Colonel. She never travelled alone before. He is interned in Japan.

On a fancy notelet for 'Baby's First Christmas' (which was David's in Klang just ten days before we fled the Japanese advance) mother added his subsequent Christmasses: the next at 'Hill Crest, Villa Erik Andrea, 4 Browns, 3 Olivers, Edith'; his third, 'Botha's Hill Hotel, Natal, 3 Browns, Nellie, Edith, Dickey'; his fourth, 'Kirkhill from Dollar'; his fifth 'Karachi, Pakistan'.

When we returned to Scotland as refugees we stayed with the Simpsons in Kirkhill (Jessie was my Godmother) and my vivid memory of that is being taken to my first pan-tomime, this becoming a Christmas tradition for several years. The two birthdays in South Africa were blessed with having family but there's a poignancy in *four* Browns for his second and then *three* Browns for his third – father had reported to the Chartered Bank in India. The Chartered was hard-pressed like every business in the war and father spent 1943-44 in Madras, 1944-45 in Calicut and 1945-47 in Karachi, with the horrors of the partition of India to cope with. He retired in 1947. Mother, having left Ian and Hamish this time with Gran in Dollar went out to join her husband, taking David, hence his fifth birthday in Karachi. By the time father received well-earned retirement and came home for good he had not see Ian for over eight years (1939-1947).

I've quite a collection of the envelopes of the letters from Father in India to us boys in Scotland, always with bulging packets of stamps, and all with them opened and inspected by the censors. The post marks give an idea of how he was moved about and on the last envelope the *Indian* stamps are overprinted *Pakistan*.

When father eventually was home for good, he bought a family home in Dollar so we boys all completed our education 'under the Ochils'. (David even returned to Dollar Academy to spend his teaching years there). On leaving school I did my two years of National Service in Egypt and Kenya (and visited Aunt Nellie in Cyprus) and, stationed by the Suez Canal, I often thought of our generation of family yo-yoing East of West and West of East. Strangely I have never gone back to the Far East while Ian, who had grown up in Scotland, spent his whole life working in Hong Kong. I did wander from the Arctic to the Andes to the High Himalaya but it was Africa and the Atlas that 'stole my heart away'. My passport after all did at one period give my profession as 'gangrel' – wanderer. Those days for me are now being nibbled away by *anno domini*, so it is time to record how it was in the Browns' most stressful years of 1939-1943. Mother never ceased saying how lucky we were compared to many. She was right of course, and whatever name is given to 'luck,' we do right to acknowledge it. Mother arrived home for good right into the severest winter in a century (1947) which must have been a contrast to the ferocious heat of Karachi. Father followed, via Cyprus to see his sister Nellie. After nine years we were all together, 'Roots at last' as Mother wrote.

In South Africa I found the big sky and the wide world I would inhabit thereafter. I roamed the Valley of a Thousand Hills with Zulu friends (hunting snakes), enjoyed Highbury School, learned to ride a bike, kept silk worms (fed from the mulberry trees in the big garden of 'Jansen's house'), had a hundred friends and a thousand joys. I could cheerfully have stayed in Natal but it, too, became another 'ending'. I could fill a book about South Africa (and would return several times as an adult) but this is the story of the family in the war. Even in South Africa it was ever present; there were other refugees arriving, news came of those killed or captured (often friends), there were uniforms everywhere, Highbury's school magazine not only listed those going on to the local senior schools (Clifton, Charterhouse!) but those who had gone on to fight and had paid with their lives. There were 'minute silences' observed all too often. We were wildly patriotic of course. I can recall an unlucky boy at school, Bellin, who was excessively blonde and therefore had to be German and was tormented with the nickname 'Berlin'.

Our chance eventually came up for repatriation. We took a flat in Durban, waiting for a ship then, thrilling for me, we made the spectacular train journey to Cape Town (the Blue Train on this route was relished years later) to join the *Andes* which had been converted into a troopship. We sailed in July 1944 and David became 'lost' before even sailing. I've a few memories of it. I can recall the vast dormitory with its tiers of bunks in which we middling-sized boys were sleeping, something like eighty of us. It was chaotic. I remember being dressed in a bulky *kapok* lifejacket for lifeboat drill. But the best memory is of having salt-water baths. The salty steaminess remains a particularly happy memory. The boys' bath I recall had big brass taps which, when turned on, nearly swooshed me out the other end of the bath. The liner relied on speed and kept well out in the oceans to avoid German submarines, (there was one call, to Freetown, Sierra Leone) before sneaking in through the North Channel to Liverpool.

The RMS *Andes* was built at Harland & Wolff and launched in March 1939, but instead of taking up her intended service to South America she was immediately converted into a troopship. In September 1945 the *Andes* brought evacuees and refugees back 'home' from Australia. Only after the war did she ply the Atlantic to South America. Later she was a Dutch cruise ship, and was finally scrapped in 1971.

I took a lot of baths and not just for the pleasure. There were medical reasons. I left South Africa with a massive crop of boils. Some suggested two pinpricks on an ankle from a snake bite might have poisoned the blood. They were big, serious boils and at one stage I could almost meet my fingers round a fibula so rotted-away was the flesh. Arriving home was quite embarrassing: I couldn't sit down. Penicillin was new then and its use retained for the military but my case was serious enough that a doctor cousin, Tom Griffith, obtained the wherewithal to treat me. This entailed an injection every four hours over several days, up one thigh and then the other, till I hated the sight of a needle. But it worked.

Years later when the *Andes* came up in conversation it uncovered perhaps the weirdest coincidence of my life. I'd reached the heights of the school's second fifteen at the time and one of the annual fixtures was with Robert Gordon's in Aberdeen. As it was considered too far to travel, play, and return to Dollar in the one day these were overnight

154

fixtures. Where possible one put up one's opposite number so, on this occasion, I hosted the Gordon's hooker. Lying in our beds chatting away, somehow the *Andes* cropped up and, slowly, a whole chain of coincidences appeared. We had both been in Malaya at the time of the Japanese invasion and been evacuated, both to South Africa, where we both went to the same school, Highbury, then both returned to Britain on the *Andes* and so to our homes in Scotland – and by the random chance of both playing hooker in our teams, we met.

Almost as weird was another coincidence with connections to our life out East. When father was old and walking something of a challenge, David and I gave him a Shetland collie, a good companion for his seaside constitutionals. After father died the dog became mine and, perforce, became a regular hill dog. He had been named Kechil, pronounced Kitchy, the Malay word for small. On one occasion Kitchy and I were heading into the hills above the Cairnwell in thick mist when I caught up a lass and we started chatting, as one does, as we continued. Suddenly she stopped and started calling "Kitchy! Kitchy!" into the mist. Astonished, I asked how she knew my dog's name and, anyway, why was she calling him? She retorted she was calling *her* dog. Before this could be taken further two dogs, *both Shelties*, came running up to us. It was a coincidence of coincidences but quite logical: both our families had been in Malaya and *Kitchy*, one of those common family-incorporated words, had been the obvious name to give to a *small* dog.

A great friend, Joan Wilmshurst (mother of the Peter born in the next bed to me in Colombo), writing to mother after father died in 1968, said, 'You always were a rather lovely person, Effie, and to be able to say "No regrets – we've been extra lucky over the years" is just you.' Dickie, writing to Ian and family after mother died in 1988 said,

155

'Aunt Effie occupied a special place in our affections ... first met back in 1942 when she, Hamish and David came through Durban as refugees. One will always treasure her cheerfulness and boundless enthusiasm for everything.' Dickie suggested in that letter that I should write something on the family history. Was the seed sown then? If so, this is my dilatory response for at least part of it, of our going east of west and west of east. Surviving. Lucky.

Notes

1. Father's bank was always a bit of a mouthful: the Chartered Bank of India, Australia and China, particularly as it never operated in Australia. Its founder was James Wilson MP (d.1860), who founded and edited *The Economist*, held various government posts and was appointed Finance Member of the Viceroy of India's Council in 1859, following the horrors of the Mutiny. The Foreign Office took over the administration of Singapore and the Straits Settlements from the East India Company thereafter.

2. In the early Nineteenth Century the German von Siebold (masquerading as a Dutchman) was the first European to glimpse Fuji and he noted people travelled and went up the 'holy' mountains not just on pious pilgrimage but for the joy and freedom of being away from everyday life. Its first ascent by an outsider was the British Minister, Sir Rutherford Alcock (1809-1897). The Swiss Consul followed suit six years later. The Rev Walter Weston was already an Alpine climber (Matterhorn, etc) when he went to Japan as a missionary in 1888 so Fuji offered nothing technical in its ascent, unlike other mountains. He was to publish *Mountaineering in the Japanese Alps* in 1896 and the Japanese Alpine Club was formed in 1894. The heaviest traffic on Fuji was, and remains,

those making a pilgrimage. There's a *torii* arch and Shinto shrine just below the summit. Japan has something like sixty active volcanoes and is prone to severe volcano activity.

3. Frank Swettenham was one of the most exotic of eastern adventurers who, oddly, had a connection with us, being a former pupil of Dollar Academy, under its first rector, the Rev Andrew Mylne. The school had been founded by one John McNabb, a poor shepherd who ran away to sea, made a fortune and founded an establishment which would offer free education for the poor of the town.

Sir Frank Swettenham was born in 1850, in Belper, Derbyshire, the youngest of a family of five siblings. When he was ten, the children and mother ran away from a 'weird' solicitor father to find refuge in Dollar, Scotland. After a year his mother died and father reappeared. Frank was sent to a boarding school in York but, money running out, returned to Dollar. With no hope of a university education he applied for a cadetship in the Straits Settlement and in 1870, aged 20, arrived in Singapore.

He soon learned to speak Malay, to become the Governor's indispensable aid in tours and meetings with Malay's rulers. Malacca (south) and Penang (north) were the 'Strait Settlements' on the long peninsula of today's Malaysia; inland lay wild jungle and wilder humans where piracy, slavery, murder and corruption flourished among the wars of succession among the local rajahs and the murderous Chinese gangster societies. After a first venture to K.L. he was posted to Penang in the north of the peninsula, on the edge of the Perak sultanate. As the best translator and enjoying social relations with the rulers he distinguished himself and steadily climbed up the bureaucratic ladder: Land Officer, then Commissioner in Perak, Assistant Resident to the Sultan of Selangor (based at Langot on the coast west of

K.L.), assistant Colonial Secretary in Singapore, Resident of Selangor (K.L.), then of Perak, becoming the first Resident General of the Malay States, second only to the Governor of Singapore, and, finally, knighted, as Governor of Singapore. Quite a meteoritic career but it rather fell to bits in the end. He had been living beyond his means for years, there were rumours of shady dealings along the way, illicit relationships, and a wife periodically driven to insanity whose divorce would terminate his position as Governor of Singapore. His happiest days had been early on, living in the back of beyond, an intellectual enjoying life with local rulers, engrossed with local culture, collecting, studying the flora, hunting, travelling as no one else ever did, all very hedonistic – and doomed as all such lives prove. Despite being the main driving force in the pacifying and development of the country his legacy was tarnished. Today, Port Swettenham is prosaic Port Kelang (Klang).

Singapore was founded – much earlier – by an equally exotic if not quixotic figure of Sir Stanford Raffles. He was born at sea off the West Indies, received little education but headed east in 1807 determined to make good. He was controversially involved in Java until 1814 when the island was returned to the Dutch. He was made Resident of Bencoolen in Sumatra thereafter but travelled extensively and pushed the East India Company to take on Singapore. The Anglo-Dutch Treaty of 1824 cleared the way for this to happen. Singapore is not a bad monument to 'the saintly merchant venturer' as Jan Morris called him.

An actual monument to him, in Singapore, was knocked down by the Japanese but was reinstalled after the war and, what's more, after Independence a second memorial to him was added. The most prestigious hotel in Singapore still has its old name, Raffle's.

He suffered ill health all his life and lost most of his family through various eastern diseases. He retired in 1823 because of this and set sail for home in a ship, *Fame*. All his belongings were aboard: furnishings, art works, a unique library, thousands of historic papers, drawings, specimens of eastern flora and fauna – and everything was lost when the ship caught fire. He faced various accusations of misconduct and, though exonerated, was still treated shabbily by the Company. His drive never ceased, he became the founder of the Zoological Society (London Zoo), was a Fellow of the Royal Society, and wrote a *History of Java*. He died of a brain tumour aged just forty five, in 1826.

4. Throughout our time in Klang mother was playing Mah Jongg regularly, an enthusiasm of many working in the East. The game is Chinese in origin and might be described as a sort of card game but played with small, beautiful tiles (144 of them) which gave it a very special aesthetic feel. Tiles were taken from a pool and discarded as cards are in many card games, working towards compiling certain winning 'sets' with the names 'chow,' 'pung' and 'kong' – which would be called out in triumph. The suits were of colourful, etched 'bamboos,' 'circles' and 'characters,' so inscribed, along with four 'dragon' tiles and four 'winds' and 'flowers'. Tiles were usually of ivory, backed by bamboo. Tiles, face down, would be mixed up (shuffled so to speak) and participants then took them to stack them in a 'wall' from which they were taken bit by bit on one's turn. Each player had a rack on which to hold his tiles as he strove to create suits. There are a couple of dice and marked scoring tokens. A beautiful travelling set returned with us to Scotland and through my teaching years of the Sixties I had kids at lunch breaks playing Mah Jongg. Their yells of 'Chow! Pung! Kong!' often puzzled passers-by, and the clicking of the tiles often took me back to those boyhood days in Klang.

160

5. Rubber trees were not indigenous but were introduced by one of the many late Nineteenth century administrators. Hugh Low, Resident for Perak was not only a notable administrator but something of a visionary, experimenting with growing coffee from Arabia, quinine from Brazil and tea from Assam. He bred cows, sheep and turkeys. In 1877 he received a dozen unfamiliar plants from Kew, to whom they had come from South America. Within a year these grew and flowered, within another were up to fourteen feet high . .. From the original dozen trees 300 seeds were to be collected (only one failed to germinate) and planted out, the first steps in what would lead to the commercial boom in rubber production. Rubber trees (*Hevea braziliensis*) originated in Brazil as the name suggested and were to be equally important in Ceylon (Sri Lanka). Klang was situated in the extensive coastal rubber belt, but they thrived in many areas. As a guide of 1927 said they had 'an endearing willingness to be good and grow quickly - for which the planter loves them'.

6. The British Army Commander General Percival would often be criticised but I've only just come on an interesting article which referred to him in 1937. Ironically, the then Brigadier A E Percival was chief of staff for a first assessment of a possible attack on Malaya and Singapore by the Japanese. They concluded the Japanese *could* easily enough capture the airfields, land in the north and advance down the peninsula – exactly as they did! They demanded greater defences in the north, a greater RAF power to defeat amphibious attacks, and the need for tanks. With these warnings unheeded Percival was handed a poisoned chalice when war came – and defeat inevitable. The ground has been gone over many times but I feel this, by Louis Allen, (*Singapore, 1941-2*) is fairest on the hapless general. 'Percival, the British Army commander, on

161

whom fell the onerous burden of an impossible battle and a humiliating capitulation, was a skilful, knowledgeable and compassionate soldier, and a man of outstanding physical courage. But the circumstances called for leadership that went beyond bravery and competence.'

Father's account and even mother's letters give understated descriptions. Some of the books listed give much more harrowing pictures of Singapore in flames, of the bloody mayhem at the wharves, of the horrors of men, women and children being bombed on their ships, and much else. Mother barely hints at the reality in letters home. That was how people behaved then – stiff upper lip, loyal and honourable.

Additional Notes:
Escaping Singapore

Evacuation from Singapore was not to be countenanced by the top brass so no plans were made, either by the top military (Lt Gen A E Percival) or civilian (Governor Sir Shenton Thomas). Over the period of 12-16 February about 5000 men (mostly military), women and children would escape Singapore and it is estimated only one in four would make it. Of forty four ships known to have left only one or two got through. Only with Singapore Island about to fall were all ships sent off in order to avoid falling into enemy hands. Japan by then had complete command of air and sea – and their planes were soon even flying out of Tengah airfield in the north of Singapore Island! Because codes had been destroyed there was no knowledge of a heavily armed Japanese invasion force in the Banka Straits by the 13th, ready for the invasion of Java. Palembang in southern Sumatra was already in Japanese hands.

This was no Dunkirk. Proportionally the casualty rate was much higher and those captured would have other hells to face. I can recommend Geoffrey Brooke's book which I only discovered after work on *East of West, West of East* was completed. It has much on Pom Pong Island and the heroics of rescues and the sad tragedies that marked the story of the many islands scattered down towards the fatal Banka Straits. Some heroes were to sacrifice their lives in repeated rescue attempts or would fall into enemy hands. A surprisingly effective escape route across Sumatra was set up via the Indragiri River, again, by a dedicated handful of military and Dutch civilians. This is a story which deserves to be far better known, surpassing by far tales of escapes in the European war. Of particular note was the work done by the many nurses and doctors among the evacuees, working with no facilities and often forfeiting their own chances of escape to attend to the wounded. (One tale had all the women present reduced to bras and pants as clothes were ripped up to make bandages).

Gilmour's book would describe Pom Pong etc having '. . . a state of affairs which defies description: men, women and children in ones and twos, in dozens, in scores and in hundreds cast upon these tropical islands within an area of say 400 miles square, of many races, of all professions (engineers, doctors, lawyers, businessmen, sisters, nurses, housewives, sailors, soldiers and airmen) all shipwrecked. Between the islands floated boats and rafts laden with people, and here and there, the lone swimmer striving to make land. All around the rafts and swimmers were dismembered limbs, dead fish and wreckage, drifting with the currents; below, in all probability, were sharks; and above, at intervals, the winged machines of death . . . It was a catastrophe beyond measure.'

One who exemplified the heroic and self-sacrificing involved was a 61 year old Australian William Reynolds, whom father mentions a couple of times, rescuing casualties from Pom Pong and then helping on the Indragiri River in Sumatra. This 'old pirate' rescued something over 1500 people from among the islands. Brooke tells what we know of this remarkable man. After a career at sea he commanded ships out of Hong Kong – and came to know the Malayan Archipelago well. When the Japanese invaded Malay he joined up with the Royal Engineers and, on the retreat down the peninsula, was demolishing anything that might have been of use to the enemy. He managed to restore a 70 foot Japanese fishing boat and escape Singapore. He arrived at Ringat on the Indragiri River towing the broken-down *Silver Gull* with 216 women and children (50 crowding his own *Kohfuku Maru* deck). He then rescued 76, some critically wounded, from Pom Pong, later taking off another 96. In eight days and nights, besides Pom Pong, he rescued survivors from the islands of Moro, Benku, Singkep and Lingga and then went on an espionage mission to distant Bintam (winning an action with a Japanese patrol vessel).

With the Japanese only 10 miles off Rengat he was ordered away. By lying up by day he worked up the Malacca Strait, between Sumatra and Malaya, rescuing yet more stragglers, travelling on to the Nicobar Islands and then made the long sea crossing of the Bay of Bengal to India and landed near Madras – 20 miles from his estimate, a voyage made with no charts or instruments beyond a simple compass. He and his ship made it back to Australia but he became involved with American intelligence and was taken by submarine to Borneo only be to be captured. He did not survive.

Reynold's boat, renamed the *Krait*, after reconstruction in Australia was used on a daring raid on shipping inside Singapore's Keppel Harbour. 39,000 tons of shipping was destroyed (Sept. 1942), the attack made using folding boats from the *Krait*. The raid was a complete success and all returned safely. The Japs went crazy and the *Kempeitai* took dreadful revenge (see Felton). (In December 1942 the better known, less successful, similar raid by the

'Cockleshell Heroes' was made on German shipping on the Gironde).

Another of the characters I was privileged to know years later, was one Lt Cdr Victor Clark. He had won a DSC at Narvik before heading to the tropical east on the *Repulse* which was then sunk two days after the Jap invasion. He was dispatched up the Malacca Strait coast of Malaya to try and rescue a brigade cut off by the advancing enemy at Batu Pahat. For four nights he and his men worked up a creek, sometimes *in* the water to move without engine noise, so close were the Japs. 2000 exhausted soldiers were ferried out safely. He gained a bar to his DSC for that exploit.

Victor set off from Singapore with 55 army personnel on 13th February (Black Friday) on HMML 311 – a 100ft Fairmile motor launch, only to be sunk in action in the Banka Straits two days later. As senior naval officer he took command when they were confronted by a Jap destroyer. A first salvo from the destroyer scored two direct hits, knocking out their one gun and killing the guncrew. Zig-zagging, they avoided further hits awhile, meantime firing at the destroyer with their Lewis guns. But the end was inevitable, with their steering broken and rudder jammed, beginning to go round in a circle, on fire, and defenceless the order came to 'Abandon ship'. Burning furiously she soon sank, White Ensign still flying. (The Japanese ship had fired 14 six-gun salvoes). The destroyer then just sailed off.

Barely twenty men, including wounded, took to the water. A group of about a dozen swimming for the shore found an abandoned lifeboat – with mast, sails, chart, compass and provisions on board and, in charge of a young P.O. (one of his crew a colonel!), sailed for 13 days through the Banka Straits only to run into a junk full of Japanese

166

soldiers. Victor had his left arm broken at the wrist but swam on alone all night, was joined by a British major, and eventually landed, alas, in mangroves. They swam along the coast and stole a canoe from an unfriendly village where they'd been joined by another officer and a private. After a week of paddling up river, paddling by day, hiding overnight, they were in a sorry state, one officer in a coma, Victor's limb swollen to 'the size of a bolster'.

The Yorkshire lad told how his Granny always made a soap and sugar poultice for any septic wound, which struck Victor as rather funny in their hapless situation but in some abandoned huts later the lad found soap and sugar and hot porridge rice and made a poultice – and it worked. The swelling subsided and pieces of shrapnel came out of the wound. The fitter pair went on. Victor made wooden splints and his arm slowly recovered over the estimated six weeks they remained hidden. Told that the Japs had been driven out of Palembang they were taken upstream by locals and through dense jungle and across the river to the town. A tiny bus picked them up – and ran them straight to the nearest barrier, guarded by the Japanese – betrayed for a reward. Victor would endure 3½ years as a P.O.W., reduced to the sort of skeletal figure one associates with Auschwitz or Belsen.

When Victor retired from the navy in 1953 he bought a boat, *Solace*, and spent several years sailing round the world in her. (His book on the voyage: *On the Wind of a Dream*). He returned to follow his vision – the building of the *Captain Scott*, a topsail schooner, which took young adult trainees on month-long Outward Bound-style courses in the stormy waters and challenging mountains of Scotland's western seaboard. They were tough challenges – and effective. I know, as I was an instructor on several winter courses and I've the letters from lads on my watches

167

saying how much the experience meant. Challenges do that. Nowhere can we see that more than in the horrors of war, in men like Victor Clark or William Reynolds or, more modestly, in my father.

The UK government hushed up the Japanese war atrocities, making released prisoners sign an undertaking not to tell of their experiences: this because of our fear of Communist China and the Soviet Union, and therefore wanting Japan as a potential ally. To this day Japan continues to hide their culpability – as if, in a similar context, Germans were never to know about the Holocaust. The British Government a few years ago granted £10,000 to the few survivors (90 year olds), while there has never been any reparation from Japan.

Bibliography

From working on this volume curiosity led me to learn a bit more of the background and the following is a selection of titles I found of interest.

Brooke, Geoffrey: *Singapore's Dunkirk* (1989) Pen & Sword edition: 2014. Illustrated. Brooke had survived the sinking of the *Prince of Wales* and after duty at Penang sailed from Singapore on the *Kung Wo* which was bombed. Survivors landed on Benku (next to Pom Pong); the stories then interlinked. The book gathers an astonishing account of many escapes and tragedies of the ships ('a Dunkirk variety') trying to escape Singapore and heading south between Sumatra and the large parallel archipelago to the east, stories of heroic duty, deeds and disasters which fully deserve their telling.

Gilmour, O W: *Singapore to Freedom* n.d [1942]. Gives an account of the *Kuala* sinking and subsequent escape: Father's story. His copy had various annotations. Photographs show Imperial Singapore as it was then.

Regan, G: *Someone has Blundered* 1987. Summaries of military and political disasters with a useful chapter on 'The Fall of Singapore'.

OTHER RELEVANT TITLES I NOTED:
Elphick, P: Singapore, The Pregnable Fortress 1995;
Warren, A: *Singapore* 2002;
Thompson, P: *The Battle for Singapore* 2005;
Smith C: *Singapore Burning; Heroism and Surrender in World War Two*, Penguin 2005.

Farrell, J. G: *The Singapore Grip* 1996. A long novel, well-researched, set in the period leading up to the Fall of Singapore. There's a good bibliography covering all aspects of the debacle.

Felton, M: *Japan's Gestapo*, Pen & Sword 2009. Reading for those with strong stomachs – on the fate of those who fell into the hands of the Kempeitai.
Kinvig, C: Scapegoat: General Percival of Singapore, 1996

NARRATIVES
Chapman, F.S : *The Jungle is Neutral.* 1949. The extraordinary story of a guerrilla fighting through the war in the Malayan jungles. A classic, 'World War Two's T.E.Lawrence'.

Keith, Agnes Newton: *Three Came Home* 1946. A touching account of a family who didn't escape and survived the horrors of internment in Borneo. 'The Japanese in this book are as war made them, not as God did, and the same is true for the rest of us'.

Lomax, Eric: *The Railway Man* 1996 (and the film based on it) is the most accessible of the many titles describing the hell the military endured on the Burma Railway and elsewhere. (Casualties numbered 12,000 POWs and 80,000 Asians).

Sim, Katharine: *Malayan Landscape* 1946. The artist wife of a Government customs officer in rural postings describes their life – and escape from the fall of Singapore.

Urquhart, A : *The Forgotten Highlander* 2010. The horrendous story of a 20 year old captured at Singapore after arriving on the *Andes,* and his slavery on the Death Railway, being adrift after his Japanese PoW transport ship was torpedoed, ending at Nagasaki when the bomb fell.

HISTORIC
Barr, Pat: *Taming the Jungle* 1977. The story of the Victorian era's 'opening up' of Malaya. Whatever judgements may be made now, this is an extraordinary picture of extraordinary men, men with virtues and vices, often ambitious and ruthless, yet frequently captivated by the strange, tough, world they transformed. (The redoubtable Victorian traveller Isabella Bird wandered from Singapore to northern jungles in 1879 and described her adventures in *The Golden Chersonese.*)

EVACUATION OF CHILDREN
Menzies, J: *Children of the Doomed Voyage*, 2005. The City of Benares tragedy.

Summers, J: *When the Children Came Home*, 2011. A chapter on the Singapore evacuees

Acknowledgements

I'm grateful first of all to my mother's copious letter-writing habit (and for other family letters), enough of which had survived to suggest this book, and for father's understated account of his horrendous escape when reporting to the Chartered Bank.

When editing the material I also did some background reading which helped to fill in my own knowledge of events and I gratefully list them in a Bibliography. Of particular note were two books directly telling father's story. Gilmour's *Singapore to Freedom* mainly concerns that misadventure as does Brooke's *Singapore's Dunkirk*, which also fully describes what the title suggests, with numerous accounts of the horrific and the heroic. Here, the escaping ships, of all sizes, set off, largely unprepared, into waters enemy-controlled, with so few escaping and so many men, women and children killed or ending up as POWs. I thank Geoffrey Brooke and Pen & Sword Books Ltd for permission to make use of their work.

As ever, my local Burntisland Library and the National Library of Scotland in Edinburgh were endlessly helpful. I also gleaned useful information from the Dollar museum through Janet Carolan, from the Dollar Academy archivist, Kirsty Molner, and from the Museum of Communication,

Burntisland. Ruth Boreham typed the much edited material and Bob Aitken added some late amendments and made final checks. David Batty read through the completed manuscript and helpfully picked up errors and infelicities. Remaining errors are mine.

Finally, my thanks to Robert Davidson and staff at Sandstone Press in Dingwall for making the book possible.